HAVE THE COURAGE TO BE DIFFERENT

RACHEL STONE

Copyright © 2022 by Rachel Stone

All rights reserved.

No part of this book may be reproduced in any form or by any electronic or mechanical means, including information storage and retrieval systems, without written permission from the author, except for the use of brief quotations in a book review.

Claim Your Freebie NOW!

Get Good At Problem Solving

Want to know the secret behind getting good at problem solving? Everyone seems to be able to do it, but you're stuck in the pile of endless to-do lists with little progress.

Ok, so how do I get my FREE book?

EASY! See the next page

Claim Your Freebie NOW

Instructions:

1. Open the camera or the QR reader application on your smartphone.
2. Point your camera at the QR code to scan the QR code.
3. A notification will pop-up on screen.
4. Click on the notification to open the website link

Contents

Introduction	ix
1. COURAGE AND PEOPLE-PLEASING	1
People-Pleasing: What is it?	2
What is the root of People-Pleasing?	6
The Spotlight Effect	9
Reasons why you should not try to please everyone all the time	10
2. UNDERSTANDING THE ORIGINS OF PEOPLE-PLEASING	14
The Compulsion to Please and to Serve	17
Fear and doubts about yourself	18
Self-Assertion and People-Pleasing are equated as good and bad	20
Fear of Conflict	21
3. REWIRE YOUR THOUGHTS	25
Rewiring your thoughts: A few general rules	26
On the presumption that you're obligated to please and serve others	26
Fear of love and acceptance	31
Is Self-Assertion bad or good?	34
It's always better to just follow others, right?	36
4. GET RID OF OUR OLD ROUTINES	42
Developing self-reliance	44
Making fewer efforts	45
Developing the ability to let go	47
Honesty is a virtue	49
Strengthening yourself when things get tough	51
Do not feel responsible for how other people feel	53
5. SET YOUR LIMITS	55
What makes a boundary?	56
When to set boundaries and how to recognise when it's time	56

How to create boundaries in your life	59
Setting boundaries: A few more steps	63
Resolving conflicts by determining boundaries	66
Consider the consequences	68
6. KNOW WHEN TO SAY NO	70
"I'm unable to" versus "I'm unwilling to"	71
Abandoning categorisation	72
"Yes. What can I prioritise less of?"	73
Maintain simplicity	74
Conclusion	79
Feedback	81

Introduction

Our direct relationships with our brains, each other, belongings, money, job, and sex are the foundations of our society. The universe is the sum of our interactions with each other and with ourselves, multiplied by six billion. Our biases, individual loneliness, selfish ambitions, physical and emotional cravings, and feelings of rage and despair are all part of who we are. Together, we are the world.

In reality, the world is nothing but ourselves. Each one of us has the power to change the world by just changing ourselves. There is a rippling effect when just one of us changes. It's contagious.

We're taught to pay attention to our instructors and parents when we're young. This makes sense from a technical standpoint. However, despite many centuries, no one has figured out how to stop themselves from suffering, much alone inflicting pain on others around them. A corresponding increase has not matched biological and scientific advancements in human psychological well-being. Everyone can learn how to earn a livelihood, but the art of living is something that each individual must discover for himself.

From loneliness, bewilderment, emotions of failure, and despair, life can be a painful experience for us. Being impoverished, mentally unwell, or experiencing violence on the street or at home may cause pain in one's life. How to cope with the shock of life's wounds is seldom taught in school. As a starting point, we are not taught that our responses to the events in our lives are the real source of our misery. The pain is caused by our fear, which stems from a need to protect ourselves. Protecting one's body is an instinct, but is it also an instinct to protect one's "self?"

Throughout our lives, we've been inspired by individuals like Susan B. Anthony, Karen Silkwood, Dian Fossey, Oskar Schindler, Rosa Parks, Nelson Mandela, and a slew of others who risked all for the greater good.

One of our favourite types is still real tales of explorers who pushed through their fears to break barriers, create records, and push the boundaries of what is possible.

When researching this book, it wasn't hard to locate stories of bravery among our fellow citizens of the 21st century. My goal was to solicit their advice on how to access and maintain one's inner strength in the face of difficulty and a sense of isolation.

Everyone seems to have a different definition of what it means to be courageous. For many people, staying in the race or donating a kidney to save a loved one was all they did to earn their place in history as heroes. For this book, the people I spoke with often said, "I don't consider myself courageous."

So, what is courage? Where can we get it, and how do we get it? When teaching our children about courage, where do we look?

After conducting a study, I determined that courage may be defined as *perseverance in the face of exhaustion, humiliation or emotional breakdown.* Indeed, everyday bravery is all about the capacity to tackle whatever life throws our way daily. What is it in a person's mind or soul that allows them to confront danger, hardship, or pain unafraid? Do you know what it means to be a person who stands firm in their beliefs?

Bravery signifies a willingness to put yourself in harm's way. When people think of bravery, heroic deeds are often the first to spring to mind. For example, entering a burning building to rescue lives is a powerful picture. After the slaughter in Tiananmen Square, there's that famous picture of the still-unidentified lone guy who stood up to the tanks of the Red Army.

Yes, we can learn a lot from these courageous efforts. But we want to know what bravery feels like for ourselves. The stories included in this book are from those who had been unemployed for months; had a loved one commit suicide; were depressed; had broken up with a partner; had relocated to a new area, and dared to stand up to a bully.

Courage, according to the author and instructor Iyanla Vanzant, is a result of acting before you are compelled to. What if we find it difficult to connect with others, such as our families or coworkers? How can we overcome our apprehension of closeness by cultivating courage? To be able to take on life's obstacles and achieve our goals, we need a source of motivation.

This capacity to face dread and suffering in danger and uncertainty is the thing we call courage, bravery, will, intrepidity or fortitude. "Physical bravery" is having the guts to go on in the face of adversity and even the prospect of death. When faced with public disapproval, embarrassment, or discouragement, moral bravery is the capacity to act by one's conscience.

In this book, I will take you inside the homes, workplaces, and hospitals of real individuals who demonstrate what it means to be courageous through their own words and deeds. In addition, I will provide advice on how to develop bravery, find your inner strength, and quit trying to satisfy everyone else.

It takes a lot of guts to go for what you really want in life. In this book, you will find the experiences of ordinary individuals who have tapped into their own bravery and fortitude in astonishing ways. They enlighten and reassure us that no matter what we dread or face, this too will pass. The tales of genuine individuals who have tapped into their bravery to live out their lives to the fullest are arguably the most meaningful. To assist you, "just do it," they serve as mentors, inspirational folks who hold your hand throughout the book.

It is my sincere hope that this book may serve as a springboard for your own brave adventure.

1

Courage and People-Pleasing

THERE IS a sense of unpredictability in the world now. Denying this new reality means we're living in denial, which puts our lives and our ability to face the difficulties in jeopardy.

The fight-or-flight reaction is often triggered by our incapacity to predict the future. We must flee and hide before fear takes hold. This is because our brains are wired to want stability and security. As youngsters, we were terrified of the bogeyman lurking in our closet, and living in uncertainty is like that. That closet door had to be opened for us to comprehend that he wasn't there.

Especially in these difficult times, where millions of people lack health insurance, are unable to pay their rent or other bills, or are terrified that they will fall ill or experience some other terrible event, we must embrace courage and draw upon the inner strength that comes from living courageously. Fortitude, strength, and resilience can only come from inside. Therefore we must open the doors of our inner closets and go out into the world.

Living boldly today is all about finding a calm strength inside ourselves that takes us through our inner fears and worries and stabilises and supports us in the face of external threats. We must learn how to shift our perspective on bravery in this new direction gently.

This chapter will look at bravery from the perspective of its earliest manifestations. "Courage" is derived from the Old French word "courage" and refers to one's inner strength and will. Some of our personal experiences have inspired us to tell others about our journeys of self-discovery, and we've also gathered tales from others who have done the same.

From researching this book and interviewing individuals who seem to be living fearlessly in these uncertain times, I noticed that most interviewees had one common trait: "I am not brave." In fact, they claimed to be terrified. Courageous individuals are those who are aware of their feelings of fear, yet they choose to take action despite them. When faced with a fear, courageous individuals face it and overcome it.

According to experts, one of the most significant skills for success is the capacity to draw into our bravery. Increasing one's bravery level may be learned, according to certain sources. Courageous individuals listen attentively to the "I believe I can, I think I can" voice within themselves, even while shaking in terror.

I don't want you to be free of fear; rather, I want you to be able to change it so that you may fully live your life even when you're facing it. If we can learn to relax and access our inner resources, we can discover optimism, creativity, and opportunity amid our most difficult situations.

People-Pleasing: What is it?

People who are generous and kind are great assets. They facilitate the exchange of ideas and information amongst individuals. Societies cannot function without them. Apathy and self-centredness lose to their methods in almost every case. These characteristics are drilled into our minds from infancy for a good reason.

People-pleasing should not be confused with charity or kindness. Individuals-pleasers and giving people may seem the same on the surface, but their motivations are quite different. People-pleasers are polite to a fault.

They're not motivated by the fact that it's the proper thing to do or because they wish to improve the lives of others. People-pleasing is motivated by insecurities, fears, and guilt rather than a genuine desire to improve.

Concerned about being rejected, the 'people-pleaser' worries. Like all of us, they need acceptance and appreciation—to be loved. On the other hand, people-pleasers are so desperate to keep their loved ones happy that they'll go to great lengths to ensure they don't lose them. They are motivated more by the want to prevent harm than by creating new possibilities. As a result of their constant fear of being rejected, they feel the need to do all in their power to avoid being rejected. It's counterproductive to please everyone, but real compassion and giving are positive actions.

At the same time, the 'people-pleaser' is looking for acceptance, which is an indication that rejection hasn't occurred. That's why they'll go to such lengths for something as simple as a thank you and a smile. People who are constantly self-sacrificing to be accepted result from a combination of these factors. Do they seem familiar to you, or do they sound like anything you've heard before?

On the appearance, people-pleasers seem to be happy in any scenario. People-pleasers don't have a care in the world. They don't seem to be bothered by anything. They always have a grin plastered on their face when others are around. Their sunny conduct certainly makes individuals around them nervous, but they believe they're doing it to make them happy. They're more open than they think, and it's hard to be around someone putting up a front. It seems dishonest at best and manipulative at worst.

Even when dissatisfied, people-pleasers never speak out about what they think, believe, or desire. When you're among people-pleasers, it's always about the other person. They'll never provide advice if they're going on a date with someone else. If they're having a difficult time, they won't say anything. They don't want to be the source of anybody else's misery or disappointment. Some people will avoid the embarrassment of standing out by merely agreeing with the group's overall opinion. They have the impression that everything is OK, regardless of how true that impression is or how accurate it is. As a result, anger festers over time, building up to the point when it erupts like a volcano.

People-pleasers will say or do anything to appease others, even if they don't mean it and/or are lying. People-pleasers are always willing to go above and above for their loved ones. In exchange for a heartfelt "Thank you very much!", they'll promise to do things their friends don't want to do or know they would make their friends happy. You're the greatest! The problem is that people-pleasers don't genuinely intend on doing these things; they claim they will to get short-term approval and make their pals happy. There's nothing they can do about the fact that their promises and inactions are irritating their pals since it becomes clear that they are prepared to lie to please others rather than tell the truth.

No matter how much they need something, people-pleasers never ask. The 'people-pleaser' pretends to ignore the importance of their wants and, as a result, will never request anybody else. They seek to portray themselves as selfless in the eyes of the public. Even if a people-pleaser musters the courage to ask for something, they will provide the person they are asking with many ways to say no. They're trying to avoid causing even the tiniest disruption or annoyance to anybody else. The 'people-pleaser' will complain about their wants not being fulfilled or handled as they brag about how unselfish they are.

As a result, why do people-pleasers engage in activities that seem dishonest and passive-aggressive?

Rejection is a fear that motivates people-pleasers, as previously stated. As a result, their people-pleasing is based more on their fear of being rejected or abandoned than on genuine emotions of friendliness. They assume that they will be less likely to be rejected or abandoned if they continue to contribute. They don't do what they do to better the lives of others; rather, they do it to boost their self-esteem.

This is not to say that all people-pleasers are evil, nasty beasts solely interested in their own desires. They have the potential to be thoughtful and kind. There is no doubt in their minds that they care deeply about the well-being of their loved ones. People-pleasers have no clue why they feel the need to please others. Moreover, they're perplexed as to why, despite their best efforts, they still feel irritated or depressed.

A person's personality or sense of identity may be reflected in various ways. You may be a people-pleaser if a couple of them seem too familiar to you.

- You are unable to say no.
- You say yes, but you mean no.
- When you agree to anything, you sulk silently in the background.
- The person who asks you to do something becomes angry when you agree.
- Many of your acquaintances and family members seem to take you for granted.
- You get the impression that the affection you've shown to others isn't being reciprocated.
- Despite all the good you're doing for others, you're feeling undervalued.
- You may be angry, resentful, misunderstood, or deceived.
- Being undesired, unloved, unvalued, or neglected makes you feel alone and lonely.
- As a result, you're concerned about offending or upsetting other people.
- You feel exhausted or worn out when you can't say no to others.
- When you do something you want to do, you feel bad.
- Instead of explaining your feelings, you assume that others will be able to discern them. When they don't, you're enraged by their indifference.
- You strive to live up to the expectations of others.
- You don't voice your thoughts or ideas, preferring instead to follow the lead of others.
- When your feelings vary from your friends or family's, you cannot openly express them.
- You take a step back from the situation and try not to become agitated.
- Defending your interests is a challenge for you.
- You're not doing the things you should be doing with a lot of vigour.

- When it comes to your feelings, you tend to keep them to yourself for fear of trouble.
- A peaceful world with no conflict between people or things is all you desire.

What is the root of People-Pleasing?

People-pleasing is no exception to the rule that habits do not form in a vacuum. People-pleasing can have a variety of basic causes, with childhood being one of the most common. But, whoever it was and whatever the situation, your penchant for people-pleasing stems from being rejected or disapproved of by someone from whom you want affirmation. It may have been your parents, teachers, classmates, abusive spouses, arrogant pals, or just plain awful people.

Those negative answers kept piling up and adding to your low self-esteem (particularly if they occurred in physical or mental abuse). That's the power of constant rejection: you'll do anything in your power to avoid it, which often means pleasing others. Being subservient and attempting to meet everyone's wishes is one approach to displaying your worth to yourself and others.

People-pleasing began in childhood. More than the religious or cultural background, the parents or guardians of the household are the most strong and present factors in any family. Parents are supposed to be our defenders, shielding us from danger, destruction, and sorrow. Children appear to love their parents unconditionally or, at the very least, rely on them for their safety.

As adults, our attitudes and behaviours are shaped by our early experiences with parents or other family authority figures. According to psychologist Hap LeCrone, people-pleasing stems from childhood or adolescence experiences where any attempts to please parents or caregivers were rejected, conditional, or otherwise unattainable.

As a result, a youngster expects praise and affirmation from his or her mother, father, or guardian. Over thousands of years of evolution, this instinct has been ingrained in us; making our parents pleased is a survival instinct.

A parent or guardian may show disapproval, possibly through

punishment, when a child does something that irritates or angers them. As a result, we see their affection as conditional. We believe our parents reject us if we don't behave the way they wish. We may regard them as emotionally unavailable or, at most, just available on rare occasions.

If we are repeatedly disliked throughout our youth, we internalise that disapproval and believe it to be who we are. We internalise that judgment as a feeling of inadequacy and inadequacy. As a result, our self-esteem and confidence suffer. After all, if the most important people in your life told you you were a duck, you'd probably believe it. It's the same with our sense of self-esteem and confidence—hearing a message too often, especially during youth, when the brain is more like a sponge, may be harmful far into adulthood.

These signals have an impact on how we perceive our adult relationships. We let others, not ourselves, decide how valuable we are: friends, bosses, and significant others. We put our own needs aside and work extra hours for them to perceive us as worthwhile persons they would never consider rejecting. However, the benefit we derive from this type of behaviour isn't real, and we can't rely on it in the long run. You may appreciate seeing the barista at your local café, but what happens when you take away his capacity to brew coffee? There's not much of a reason to spend time with him.

Emotional neediness: Another typical reason for people-pleasing is to please others. When you are overly reliant on another person, whether your spouse, significant other, or friend, you are said to be co-dependent. We genuinely care about them and strive for their acceptance. We might, however, cultivate the concept that love is conditional, that it will only be given to us if we meet all of someone's criteria and behave in the way they desire. We may be afraid of desertion or rejection, so we try to win others' affection by becoming good boys and girls. We believe that if we consistently delight someone, they would love and accept us for whatever we do for them.

These attitudes and behaviours are signs of co-dependency, which explains why some of us are such sticklers for pleasing others. We are afraid of disappointing them, so we do everything we can to make them happy so that they will continue to like us. It's an instinct, but it's also unbalanced and stressful.

Never arguing: People-pleasing might evolve in this way over time. Pity-pushers would never say anything that would put us all in danger. We never argue about where to eat or what to eat with the other person, even if we don't agree with their points of view, and we just "go with their flow" to avoid conflict. Ultimately, any disagreement is an opportunity for a person to be rejected. We also avoid confrontation because we don't know how painful the reaction or backlash will be.

In the grand scheme of things, what we need or want pales compared to what everyone else wants or needs. Instead of expressing our thoughts and feelings, we rely on the opinions of others. It's not uncommon for spouses to promote and validate their partner's political beliefs, even if their views are very different or even opposing. To keep their relationship intact, they're hesitant to express their opinions. Even though this is rarely done on purpose, the desire to please is a universal human trait.

Is it time to move on? For those who have an agenda against us, our prior troubles (especially those from our formative years) may be construed as an excuse. Exactly how long did it take you to overcome it? Instead of dragging this out, why not just let it go?"

They probably don't understand how absurd such insistence sounds because it's another type of rejection.

It's not only impossible to overcome it quickly, but you also don't have a choice. Traumas and mistreatment, in particular, have long-term impacts that do not go away after the source of the trauma or mistreatment are removed. If you believe what John Sarno says in his book **The Divided Mind**, the feelings you have in your unconscious mind throughout your life, including your childhood, are permanent. You'll carry the anger, hurt, emotional suffering, and sadness you felt as a youngster into adulthood.

They always show up in our relationships because they are so deeply rooted. We are drawn to people who exaggerate our worst characteristics and weaknesses unconsciously. Relationships allow us to relive our past experiences in some way. It's common for people-pleasers to place themselves in a submissive position when they hand over control to others. To say that one can't learn to live and prosper in the presence of these memories and effects is an understatement; nonetheless, our unsympathetic friends would have us believe that we can. That's a stretch, to put it mildly.

The Spotlight Effect

Most of us tend to believe that we are constantly being observed. We tend to believe that everyone in our social circle is evaluating our appearance and behaviour because the boundaries of our perspective confine us. The spotlight effect is a false sense of self-importance that can harm our personal and interpersonal connections. The thought that everyone would witness how awful a dancer we are makes us hesitant to go out and have some fun.

Daily, the spotlight effect makes us feel dumb and humiliated because it distorts our perceptions of reality. Assuming everyone is watching and recording our every move and reaction, we're certain that they're secretly laughing at, criticising, or berating us. To avoid further embarrassment, we tend to over-modulate our conduct or even withdraw completely from the public eye.

The spotlight effect, on the other hand, is purely fictitious. Because it isn't "scalable," for one thing, no one can care about another person's life if they're all focused on their own. If you're lucky, only a few people keep an eye on your every move, and they're likely to be folks you've already developed a close relationship with. Even they, however, are not exempt from the need to attend to their concerns.

In general, the public isn't interested in your every move unless you're a celebrity, such as a rock star or a popular figure on social media. Your perception of how closely the world is watching you may be substantially distorted even if you are a famous figure.

There is still an issue with the spotlight effect, and it considerably worsens the situation for people-pleasers. They're already worried that they won't meet other people's expectations. That's compounded by the spotlight effect, which causes them to feel as though the rest of the world is constantly scrutinising them. They're desperate to make up for any wrongdoing, to do whatever it takes to keep any criticism or rejection at arm's length. Concern quickly escalates to full-blown terror. When they don't act quickly to correct an issue, they fear the entire group will reject them.

It's important to move outside of your comfort zone to determine whether or not others are noticing you. Pay attention to how other people react to what you're doing and how they react to them. You'll be able to take a break from your anxiety due to this, which solves a large portion of the issue. For one thing, you'll learn just how little of an impact your every move has on others.

Reasons why you should not try to please everyone all the time

When you're always pressured to satisfy others, it negatively influences your mental and emotional well-being.

Self-indulgence: When you're preoccupied with meeting the expectations of others, you forget to take care of your own needs. You may be overlooking or ignoring what you need to do to care for yourself. Everything from working out to paying the bills to just having fun could fall under this category. Because of a looming deadline, you find yourself working into the early hours of the morning to fix an issue that could have been dealt with the following day. When a family issue arises that isn't an emergency; you can skip a workout to attend to it.

If you have mental or emotional troubles, they can easily evolve into physical health concerns. You need to be able to balance your interests with the interests of others.

Disturbance, hostility, and passive aggression: When you place yourself in an inferior position to everyone else, you'll automatically build resentment toward others around you. This resentment can come in the form of cutting remarks or disdainful jokes after spending so much time pleasing others. This kind of passive-aggressive behaviour can do more harm than good in the long run.

If you want to please others, you must nurture an attitude of giving and selflessness, which will only bury more unpleasant emotions like fury, anguish, and hatred further into your soul. There's no doubt about it, if these bad feelings aren't acknowledged and dealt with, they'll manifest themselves in harsh, possibly violent ways. An emotional and mental breakdown, as well as a physical one, are all possibilities.

Consider the case of a submissive spouse who must put their plans on hold to meet their partner's needs. After a few months of silent simmering, the spouse may have to deal with resentment that they can't do what they want, and it all bursts out in an unexpected rage against their partner.

An inability to take pleasure in one's surroundings: You can't enjoy life if you're always thinking about what you need to do for others, and that's a given. When you're preoccupied with the happiness of others, it's hard to put your attention on your well-being. You won't be able to enjoy a delicious meal, a weekend road trip, or your child's football match because you'll be so fatigued. Because of this, your friends and family will be able to read your displeasure right off your face. What are you teaching your children when you simply show up for them but appear entirely disengaged and disconnected? This can have a significant impact on their development.

Depressive and anxious states: When you have too many requests on your time, you're in the grips of stress. It's impossible to meet everyone's expectations when striving to please everyone all of the time. Unmet expectations quickly lead to depression, and it becomes difficult to break free of this vicious cycle. Your to-do list is never-ending, and it's always becoming longer as you add tasks for others.

Because of the excessive effort required to achieve the expectations that a people-pleaser perceives as being placed on them, these individuals are constantly under a great deal of pressure. An individual may fall into profound despair only to emerge from it with a fresh round of people-pleasing, as they've worn themselves out improving the lives of others but haven't experienced any success in their own right. That's how things function in a cycle.

The act of taking advantage of another person: If you gain a reputation for being a people-pleaser, you put yourself at risk of being used. This could lead to a rise in the number of requests you receive from people who think you're willing to do anything for them. Selfish and exploitative people will take advantage of your flaws without hesitation. Even those who aren't malicious won't be able to tell if you're overloaded and will have unrealistic expectations of what you can give.

In the workplace, this problem is particularly significant. Your workload may be excessively burdened by a senior executive who is more concerned with earnings than your well-being. Eventually, one of your coworkers, who is usually a nice guy, will notice how well you handle various jobs and will start considering you the "go-to" person for all types of stuff. Due to your calm demeanour, they have no idea you're being misused and spending your nights at the office.

The desire to be in charge: People-pleasing is viewed as generous and selfless behaviour. On the contrary, it's more self-serving. When you try to please everyone, you're attempting to control the thoughts, feelings, and behaviours to repay emotional debt. The way you're attempting to impose control over their lives and situations is truly shady and underhanded. We go out of our way to please and serve others because we desire a specific outcome. We desire a reservoir of emotional debt that maintains us in the good graces or circle. If this sounds manipulative, you're not alone. An initial desire to be in charge quickly turns into a full-blown obsession.

Nobody knows who you are: To maintain their image, people-pleasers pay the price. People don't know who you are because you've done such a good job at hiding your emotions. There is only one thing they know about you: your persona for getting along with others. Instead of bringing you closer to others, your desire to be loved and adored by everyone will isolate you and make you appear hollow and unauthentic.

Eventually, the "true" you will emerge, and it may be a lot more ugly than you expected. You could be afraid of getting drunk to avoid revealing all of your secret thoughts and ideas, especially sarcastic remarks about the individuals you've been attempting to please all along. Instead of being blunt and rude, you could have conveyed your displeasure more politely (and maybe solved it ahead of time).

. . .

A DESIRE TO please others is not the same as showing kindness or generosity. It's not something you do out of genuine compassion for humanity or the well-being of your family. Our urge to please others stems from unhealthy emotional gaps and the desire to please ourselves rather than from a desire to please others. It's much easy than you might think to recognise the difference between fake friendliness and true compassion, and those who have been exposed as people-pleasers don't get much respect. In addition, they don't see themselves as highly as they should.

Nevertheless, despite all the compelling evidence against it, we continue to engage in this practice. To stop this, we need to figure out what drives people-pleasing—where the conviction that we need to do it comes from. This will be the subject of the next chapter.

2

Understanding the origins of People-Pleasing

You notice someone cutting ahead of you in line. That can't be right, you realise. If the individual in question doesn't know where they're going, you have every right to point them in the right direction. Your gut clenches and your throat feels lumpy at the notion of speaking out, but you can't bring yourself to do it.

It's too much for you to bear. Rather than causing a scene, you decide it's best to let the situation go. You feel the stress in your body dissipate, your stomach relaxes, and your throat unclogs due to this decision. That's much more satisfactory.

You may recognise these feelings if you're a people-pleaser or someone who is constantly concerned that they lack confidence in their own opinions. There are times in your life when it's hard for you to say no to people's demands or when you're presented with a scenario that requires you to prioritise or assert yourself in some way, and you feel these sentiments.

But how well do you remember the script's backstory, even if you're familiar with the scene that plays out on such occasions? What if you looked behind the curtain to discover the roots and causes of these tendencies toward self-denial? In situations where you have to stand up for yourself, say no, or refuse others, what may be the cause of your overwhelming tensions and negative feelings?

This chapter will explore the underlying mechanisms that underlie people-pleasing and non-assailant behaviours, even when such actions prove harmful to the persons who engage in them. Rather than blaming childhood traumas for these tendencies, the truth is a more nuanced mix of psychological concerns, skewed perceptions, and irrational worries. They may be rooted in a person's upbringing, but more often than not, they result from the person's current environment or habits they have developed on their own.

Consider Emily's situation. As the oldest of four children in a home without a father, Emily learned early on the importance of taking charge of her future.

Since a very young age, the ability to sense what other people need and want even when they don't express it has been a life skill for her, and she's dedicated her life's work to making sure those desires are met. She helped her mother out around the house, worked part-time while she went to school, and raised her younger siblings as if they were her own. Over time, this pattern of behaviour began to affect her personal and professional relationships and her love relationships. Every time someone needed help, a stand-in, or just someone to listen, she was the first person they called.

Having no time for herself was considered a badge of honour, a sign of her dedication and devotion to those she cared about.

With two young children, Emily is still steadfast in her opinion that being a good wife and mother involves constantly prioritising the needs of others. As a full-time employee, she also takes care of her husband and children, and she feels humiliated if she needs help with housework.

In her mind, she's accountable for everything from updating the grocery list to making everyone happy and content. There are so many things on her to-do list and responsibilities that she feels terrible about having time for herself, such as exercising, getting regular health checkups, spending time with friends, or just relaxing.

Many physical illnesses, from the ordinary cold to migraines to stress ulcers, eventually become increasingly prevalent for Emily. Despite this, she feels guilty about getting unwell because she cannot carry out her professed mission, which is to care for others rather than being cared for herself.

However, the underlying issue isn't their tendency to please others for those like Emily. As with skin bruises that appear due to tissue trauma, these behaviours are just the apparent indications of underlying disorders. This means that people-pleasing does not constitute the root of the problem.

People-pleasing conduct may have several causes. Four, in particular, have a habit of poking their heads out from time to time.

Some people have the misguided notion that helping others comes naturally while looking out for one's interests comes last. When it comes to relationships, the more one-sided they may be, the better. They may have developed a habit of putting others before themselves. A strong sense of guilt might easily keep you from doing anything else if this is your belief.

The second problem is that many people-pleasers have concerns about their self-worth. Only by saying yes to everything that is asked of them can they gain a sense of self-worth and a shot at acceptance.

Many people are eager to please think of it as a form of charity and morality to please others. Saying no and asserting one's independence, on the other hand, are equated with harshness and badness. Because they are so focused on maintaining their "good" reputation, they are easy prey for scammers.

Finally, many people-pleasers act the way they do because they are afraid of confrontation. Rather than risk upsetting the apple cart, they would rather hold their tongue until they were blue in the face, leading to a life of resentment and suppressed feelings.

This chapter primarily discusses the four root causes of the alleged sickness of pleasing. Identifying the root causes of a problem in your personal or professional connections is critical if you've become afflicted with this illness.

Knowing why you behave the way you do will help you break free of this predisposition toward people-pleasing. In this section, you will learn how to identify the mindsets that you need to alter and how to implement specific solutions and concrete activities that will work best for you in your particular circumstance. Take some time to study the following specific causes of people-pleasing before moving on to the next steps in quitting this self-destructive habit.

The Compulsion to Please and to Serve

Since you were a child, you've probably been taught that putting others before yourself is always the better course of action. You were rewarded with praise because of your generosity in sharing the cookie pack with your brother or allowing that other kid to play on the swing after you. As for you, you were chastised whenever you refused to share or put others first.

You may have developed a false idea that you're never allowed to put yourself first because of these teachings and experiences—for example, those of generosity and compassion—which are imprinted in them.

You've come to believe that you should constantly put others before yourself, to the point that doing things for yourself causes you to experience severe guilt. It doesn't even matter that these activities are anticipated or important for your health. As a result of your upbringing, you've been conditioned to believe that doing these things for yourself is a reason for self-criticism and shame. To avoid the guilt of putting yourself first, you feel compelled to satisfy and serve others instead.

Standing up for yourself and refusing others may seem counterintuitive if you've grown up believing that your whole goal in life is to satisfy others. You expect to always put others before yourself to uphold generosity and kindness. To avoid upsetting or disappointing others, you experience a great deal of guilt, which you interpret as evidence that you've transgressed some fundamental moral norm. You take that overwhelming sense of shame as a warning that rejecting others and placing your own needs ahead of others is wrong and that you should always prioritise others.

For instance, Noah is a dedicated leader who is always willing to bear the blame for the mistakes of his employees. In his mind, everyone on his team is under his authority as a leader, and if they don't do their jobs, he'll have to do them himself. He feels a great deal of guilt if he cannot meet the requirements of any of his family members or deal with any of their issues since he believes that he is expected to be the go-to person for any problems.

He avoids confronting his employees about poor performance or even misbehaviours because he is afraid of what would happen if he does so. As a result, he works harder than ever to make up for any mistakes and make sure everyone on his team is happy, even sacrificing time with his family or personal life. Noah feels guilty about prioritising himself over his coworkers because he believes it is his obligation as a leader to put them before himself.

To put it another way, in addition to feeling guilty about prioritising oneself, the great drive to please and serve others stems from a sense of responsibility for others' feelings and behaviours.

If you refuse to help a buddy because you don't want to make them feel guilty or ignored, you think it's your fault.

If only you had yielded to what they wanted, you felt responsible for every disillusioned expression or disappointed gaze. For the sake of others, you're willing to sacrifice your happiness and mental well-being to keep everyone else happy and calm. One of the signs you're taking good care of your connections with others is your willingness to go out of your way to keep everyone pleased.

Such an attitude has the unfortunate effect of distorting our understanding of what makes for a good relationship. Healthy relationships are possible with a good balance between consideration for others' needs and making sure you don't overlook your own. Working to improve the lives of those around you is admirable—but not at the expense of your well-being and contentment.

Fear and doubts about yourself

Insecurities and a lack of self-worth are two other important causes of people-pleasing behaviour. When you have a lot of self-doubts and low self-esteem, you believe that rejection is inevitable and that you deserve it. Your lack of interest in others, much less their approval or love, makes it impossible to comprehend why anyone would care about or even like you.

You have a deep-seated belief that you aren't good enough and that you aren't worthy of love, which causes you to be on the lookout for rejection constantly. To avoid being rejected, you become highly sensitive to any signs of it, including a frown or an offhand remark of disappointment from those you are trying to avoid.

As a result of this anxiety and fear of being rejected, you become a people-pleaser because you believe that you are only valuable if you please or serve others as they desire. Your lack of faith in the ability of others to appreciate your unique qualities has led to a constant search for validation and affection outside of yourself.

To protect yourself from the pain and humiliation of others' dissatisfaction and rejection, you do whatever it takes to keep your fragile sense of self-worth intact.

Let's say you're the daughter of Rosie, a lady who's spent much of her life attempting to win her mother's unconditional love by behaving in a submissive or obedient manner. Rosie, now a wife and mother, finds herself unwittingly re-enacting the same patterns of interactions with the people around her. She is concerned that her children will find out she is a bad mother if her husband stays with her, thinking he is doing her a favour by sticking with her.

She neglects her own needs to satisfy her insecurities and feelings of worthlessness. She only accepts their affection if they are pleased with her actions.

Not many people are willing to admit that they have ever felt unloveable. Many of your behaviours—including people-pleasing—are motivated by something you're unaware of, like an invisible but profound wound you're carrying around with you. It's possible that you were aware of it even before you reached puberty. Your parents may have always favoured a sibling or a friend over you, and you've managed to convince yourself that you're not as good as them.

You've come to believe that you're unworthy of love and acceptance since so many other individuals are better than you.

At your core, you believe you're not worthy of the love given to you voluntarily and without conditions. While you may not be deserving of the love you're now receiving, you may be able to win it by constantly striving to be better, give more, and serve more.

As a result, you've developed the habit of pleasing and serving others to acquire their love, even while you feel unworthy of it. You regard pleasing others as the answer to those deep wounds of insecurity and self-worthlessness that you've been nursing.

Self-Assertion and People-Pleasing are equated as good and bad

From the time a child is a baby, the value of being a decent person is instilled in them by parents and teachers alike. "Play kind," "Be kind," and "Be good" are probably some of the first pieces of advice your parents ever gave you as a kid.

The terms "pleasant," "kind," and "good" are frequently used interchangeably, leading some to mistake them for black-and-white categories of behaviour. A person who thinks they must be polite all the time to be a good person, such as denying a favour or pointing out someone who infringes on their rights, is considered bad. There isn't the same level of remorse here as there is in the desire to help others. In reality, it's just a misguided view of how relationships should be.

People-pleasing behaviour results from thinking that links being kind with being a good person and asserting oneself with being a bad person. When it comes to this issue, those who are most likely to be ardent people-pleasers are those who believe that they must be perceived as nice people by everyone. Your reputation as a pleasant and good person means a lot, and if you care about it, you'll spend a lot of time and effort trying to please everyone.

There should be no one in your life who is dissatisfied with your conduct since one slip-up can destroy the flawless nice-person image you've been working so hard to maintain. Is this what you came up with? People-pleasing and non-assertive behaviour at the highest levels.

Charlie has always taken great delight in being a good friend and a good person. To him, he is defined by these characteristics and does everything in his power to live up to that image. He agrees to lend a large sum of money to a buddy, despite knowing that he cannot afford to do so. In his mind, telling someone no makes him a lousy friend, and he doesn't want to be that.

The bottom line is that for Charlie, being a good friend means doing everything it takes not to be that horrible person. He doesn't want to risk losing the money he's lending to his friend. Because of that, he avoids making some essential purchases for a few months, accruing late fees and interest charges that he now has to pay on his own. To avoid making a terrible impression on his friend, he must accept the consequences.

There is nothing dishonourable in a wish to be a decent person or perceived as a pleasant person. However, the concept that you can't stand up for yourself while also being a good or pleasant person is incorrect. To be aggressive when necessary is entirely OK, and it won't make you a bad person for doing so. It's also a misconception to believe that being altruistic all the time makes you a wonderful person.

If you utilise selflessness indiscriminately rather than out of real care for others, you risk turning it into a vice rather than a virtue.

In contrast, selfishness is a principle that should be revisited and practised in moderation despite its bad connotations. When viewed from a fresh perspective and used appropriately, selfishness can benefit.

This is a positive type of selfishness, one that is important to preserve your health and restore your energy before you give of yourself to others and avoid spreading yourself too wide by catering to everyone else's needs. You must indulge in this kind of self-indulgence without guilt to achieve your own goals, desires, and well-being. By allowing yourself to be selfish from time to time, you'll be able to better watch out for others and share the joy you experience with them.

Fear of Conflict

When it comes to people-pleasing, it may stem from fear of confrontation. To keep everyone happy, you must be willing to go along with everyone else's wishes, and you will never dare to say no or stand up for yourself if you're afraid to rock the boat. People-pleasing is the result of a collection of these dispositions and practices.

To avoid being a doormat or a pushover because you're hesitant to express yourself, you need to overcome your apprehensions about speaking up for yourself. You may not always be conscious of how your actions are motivated by a fear of confrontation.

Even if people-pleasing is rooted in fear of conflict, that fear's foundation may still be deeper. You may be reluctant to speak up about what you want because you believe you won't be heard. If you don't succeed in your quest to have your rights acknowledged, you may be afraid of being humiliated due to your efforts to stand up for yourself.

Your reputation, work, or even a relationship could be on the line if you engage in a conflict. When confronting someone, you may fear that you or the person you're confronting will experience unpleasant or even uncontrollable feelings like guilt, wrath, or disdain. As a result, you're concerned that confronting your partner will simply make things worse and that you won't be able to manage it.

There's a way to keep things from getting worse, and it involves doing what you think is the simplest thing possible: not saying anything, refusing something, or confronting someone. Inaction is fine if that's what it takes. Your remedy is to learn how to delight others.

This is a good time to think about what you'd do in a workplace where you feel your ideas are swiftly brushed aside, even though you have valuable talents and more years of experience than your colleagues. However, you're scared that telling your boss about your concerns would make you appear pompous or that she'll believe you're challenging her delegation abilities, leading to her being angry at you. In other words, you are paralysed from speaking up for yourself for fear of jeopardising your professional reputation and connection with your manager.

When you avoid conflict, it doesn't necessarily mean you don't want to talk about your problem with others. When there's a discrepancy between what's required of you and what you want to do, you're more likely to seek conflict. As a result, you avoid confrontation because you're terrified of the prospective consequences.

As a result, the urge to confront others often manifests itself in other, often ugly and harmful ways. Passive-aggressive behaviour is expressing one's feelings rather than expressing them explicitly.

Passive-aggressive acts are indications of hate that are often unintentional. When a coworker asks you to make a report for her, you may not have explicitly stated no, but you conveniently forget to convey your anger at being asked to do so. Instead of telling your spouse that you're not upset that he didn't phone you once while on business, you might pretend you're not and then "forget" to let him know where you've been for the rest of the week.

The relationship suffers from your attempts to avoid conflict by engaging in passive-aggressive behaviour, which undermines the goodwill you've worked so hard to maintain.

As a result, avoiding conflict out of concern that it will only make things worse leads to the precise outcomes it is attempting to prevent. Contrary to popular belief, the fact that a couple hasn't fought for a while does not imply that their relationship is in good shape. You can't have good interpersonal relationships if you can't overcome your fear of confrontation and learn to deal with disagreement more effectively.

Even if you think you're flexible and adaptable, you're bound to run into conflict since you're a unique individual with unique views, feelings, desires, and values that may or may not coincide with other people's. To maintain healthy relationships with others (and with yourself), you must be able to tolerate disagreement and overcome your fear of confrontation.

Pleasing others can be difficult to break because it isn't selfish. When people thank you for every favour you provide and every violation you allow to go unpunished, it can make you appear more pleasant and honourable. It can even reward you with emotions of contentment from time to time.

People-pleasing may seem like a good idea at first glance, but if you dig deeper, you'll discover that it's narcissistic and self-destructive. If you're only interested in pleasing others, you're likely harbouring a host of negative emotions, such as insecurities and a sense of worthlessness, as well as misconceptions about what it means to be a good person or a paralysing fear of conflict.

Is it truly worth living your life this way, tethered to the self-destructive habit of constantly being at the service of others?

If the answer to this question is "no," it's time to stand on your own two feet. Breaking people-pleasing begins with an awareness of its root causes. To move forward, you need to learn how to stand up for yourself, say no to other people, and generally cease the people-pleasing frenzy you've let run your life for too long—in other words, it's time to learn how to treat yourself properly.

3

Rewire your thoughts

IN THE LAST CHAPTER, we looked at the underlying ideas that drive people-pleasing activities, such as the idea that living your life to please and serve others is a negative thing, that you're unworthy of love just the way you are, and that voicing your own opinions implies you're a nasty person.

People-pleasing is a logical consequence of having such skewed perspectives on the world and yourself. You've allowed yourself to believe that you're deficient rather than feeling whole and complete as you are. You've grown dependent on the acceptance of others to fill the void left by a lack of healthy self-esteem and self-love. To the detriment of your relationships with others and yourself, your distorted attitudes and beliefs have contributed to this.

If you want to free yourself from the compulsion to please others, you'll have to profoundly change your perspective on the world and, maybe more crucially, on yourself. Change your behaviour by retraining your underlying beliefs and views, especially those that influence your tendency to put others first and yourself last. This section is all about providing you with the skills to achieve precisely that.

Rewiring your thoughts: A few general rules

It's not easy to change your viewpoint. People-pleasing beliefs and behaviours can become part of one's identity because they are linked with one's personal history, critical events, and general temperament. In a sense, your actions reflect your beliefs, your beliefs reflect your experiences, and your experiences reflect your beliefs.

As a result of the difficulty in separating who you are from your views, a simple activity like changing the flooring in your home may be easier than altering your worldview. Because it is more tangible, easier to control, and hence necessitates less willpower and self-control on your side, hard labour is an appealing option for many people. However, is it possible to alter your viewpoints? That's a tougher problem to solve. There is a lot of mental, abstract, and fluid work involved in modifying your thoughts about the world and yourself. It also necessitates a great amount of focus and devotion.

However, even though altering your views is tough, it is not unattainable. If you're willing to put in the effort, you can change your views to become a better version of yourself by learning the best practices.

Cognitive behavioural therapy (CBT) is a tried-and-true method for altering one's mindset. According to this strategy, you can modify your behaviour by changing the way you think. Learn to recognise the thoughts you have and distinguish them from those that are real and those that aren't. Then attempt to replace those thoughts with those that are true.

On the presumption that you're obligated to please and serve others

Being self-centred is never a good thing. One of the foundations for a lifetime of people-pleasing habits is this idea, typically pounded into our heads since childhood. When you're taught as a child that putting oneself first is equated to being a bad person, you build a mentality that forces you to put others first.

A simple playdate may have sowed the seeds of this kind of thinking in you at a young age. In the end, your mother may have told you to let go of your prized possession and learn to share since that's what good children do. You were praised for being kind after doing what you were taught. Once you've discovered the benefits of putting others before yourself, you'll continue to do so to win others' acceptance and love.

The other side of the coin is what happens if you decide to put yourself first instead of following the core lesson. When you were a kid, you might have pushed the limits of politeness by refusing to let someone else have your favourite toy. You may have been swayed by various tactics, such as being told how unhappy you're making the other kid feel or being labelled a bad child, to give up on asserting yourself. This teaches you that prioritising yourself is wrong and should make you feel bad. Eventually, as an adult, you realise that putting yourself first, especially when it comes to things like prioritising your health, isn't the best way to go about things.

"Don't be selfish" is an innocent aphorism, but it often turns into a self-destructive belief that putting yourself first makes you a bad person if you're not careful. People-pleasing habits are hard to quit because they are fuelled by feelings of guilt and approval that come from putting others before oneself.

People-pleasing habits can only be broken by rethinking your definition of selfishness. When we say we are being selfish, we simply mean placing our interests above others. Rather than ignoring your own desires to please others, self-worth comes from being aware of your desires and honouring them. It's not necessarily a negative thing to be self-centred. For the following reasons, it is vital to be selfish from time to time.

To give your all to others, you must first give your all to yourself. Doing good deeds for the sake of others and nurturing your connections is perfectly acceptable. Nevertheless, moderation is essential in all endeavours, even when it comes to lofty pursuits like service and reliability. At some point, putting others first becomes detrimental to everyone involved, not just you.

Many people-pleasers fail to comprehend that sacrificing so much of themselves to serve everyone else around them is destroying their capacity to continue to be there for others when it truly matters.

When you're continually drained and frazzled, sleep-deprived, and stressed out from taking care of everyone else, you're more likely to fall ill, lose interest in work, or simply become uninterested in any of those things. You will gradually lose the ability to serve others with genuine care and pleasure if you don't get adequate sleep, food, and rest. In a strange paradox, serving those you want to please is impossible if you are too selfless.

Evie, for instance, is a hardworking mother who also happens to be a dedicated business leader. She gives up sleep, skips meals, and other forms of self-care to better serve her family and her job, all in the name of being a selfless homemaker and professional. With her poor lifestyle choices, she develops serious stress ulcers, and she ends up in the hospital for surgery and bed rest. In her effort to assist everyone around her, she realises that she is unable to accomplish much for anyone.

You must learn to prioritise yourself and be a little selfish where it counts to put others first and give yourself meaningfully truly. The best way to ensure that you can continue to be there for your loved ones when they need you most is by prioritising your health and well-being. So, by being self-centred, you may progressively regain your self-esteem and use this newly acquired energy to improve your performance in any endeavour you choose. A good rule of thumb is that you'll be better off in the long run if you're operating at 100%.

You are the only person in charge of your well-being. Selfishness is essential since you are the only one who can properly care for yourself. These are all activities that others can take, but they are not actions you can take. You have to accept responsibility for your health and well-being. You are the only one who can eat a nutritious diet, exercise regularly, and pay attention to your body's warning signs when it's time to consult a doctor. Your entire survival is in jeopardy if you ignore these things to please everyone else.

Keep in mind that no one else will be able to assist you with these tasks. Since they aren't you, they can't feel your pain in the same way you can. No matter how much we hope for it, no matter how much we pray for it, our parents and siblings will never be able to give you the attention and care you deserve. You are the only one who can do these things for yourself, so don't feel guilty about it. Self-preservation takes precedence over pleasing others. Daily, it's easy to forget that our ultimate purpose is self-preservation.

Selfishness does not imply irresponsibility or disrespect for others. Taking a half-day break from chores on the weekend doesn't make you a lazy person. If you were unable to attend your friend's party, it doesn't imply you've abandoned them for good and never will. To take care of yourself, you may have to reduce the amount of time you spend with other people.

Be ok with saying no to social engagements if that is what you need to refuel your batteries. You can't view selfishness as completely negative because the world doesn't operate in black and white. It's a long way from the truth. Because of the negative connotations of the word "selfish," we are socialised to avoid engaging in it. The worst way to be selfish is to be driven by egotism and to just look out for your interests at the expense of others. Indeed, this kind of selfishness is harmful rather than helpful. However, this is the exception rather than the rule, and it has little to do with the topic at hand.

As long as we don't cause harm to anyone else, we're happy. We're merely urging you to put your own needs above those of others from time to time. Selfishness like this can help you break the cycle of self-destructive people-pleasing you've fallen into. There are two basic ways to be selfish deliberately and the tips above on how to tackle your thoughts about selfishness (in a good way).

Give attention to your physical well-being. Physical health suffers when you are constantly trying to satisfy others. If you have a lot of duties at home and work, you'll have a hard time getting enough sleep, exercising, and eating healthily because you'll have no time or energy to do so. Continuing in this manner is a surefire way to contract a wide range of illnesses, from the ordinary cold to heart disease. People-pleasers can end up dying due to their continuous efforts to please others.

You owe it to yourself to prioritise your health before allowing any damage to your body that cannot be reversed. Use that as a new filter whenever you're faced with the choice of prioritising yourself or others. Is this going to hurt your health? Does it have the potential to cause you to neglect your health in the long run? If that's the case, you'll have to take a pass on that. If someone's request interferes with your workout or sleep schedule, this is a good metric to keep you from bending over backwards.

Saying no to requests will allow you to set aside time to prepare and consume nutritious meals, get adequate sleep and rest, and exercise regularly. Prevent social obligations from interfering with the time you set aside for self-care tasks like these by scheduling them specifically in your daily routine. It's yours and yours alone when it comes to these blocks of time. Learn to tell folks you can't do something or attend a gathering because you need to work out, do some grocery shopping, or just rest. Get used to saying no. Being selfish is vital since your physical health puts everything else at risk when you're in danger.

Set your thoughts in order of importance. Because of the numerous stresses of modern life, the concept of self-care has expanded to include not just physical well-being but also emotional well-being and mental clarity. This is another way to determine if you should do something or not: does it make you unhappy, tense, or uncomfortable mentally?

It's the weekend, and you're invited to your friend's large party. Because you know your friend so well, you know that the party will be raucous and packed, everything you don't like. The best thing you can do for your mental health is politely but firmly decline the offer if you know you won't enjoy yourself there. Rejecting the invitation is not the same as rejecting your friend, and taking a relaxing weekend to focus on yourself is perfectly acceptable.

To the extent that you're a "people-pleaser," you're prone to ongoing psychological pain. Confidence and self-worth issues are common among them; they also suffer from excessive worry and guilt when they decline others' invitations, unreasonable expectations of themselves, and misguided ideas about what it means to be a good person. Additionally, they may feel self-conscious about their physical or mental health. If assisting someone else causes you to feel bad feelings, it should be a no-brainer for you.

Self-respect and the ability to be one's own best friend can be learned. Learn to recognise and reject self-defeating and hurtful attitudes that say you're not good enough for love and approval until you do exactly what others desire. Do your best to avoid the things and people that trigger those feelings. People who genuinely care about you and accept you for who you are will do so without conditions. Just because you declined their request or asserted yourself, they won't reject or withdraw their affection from you.

The most important thing to remember is to quit beating yourself up for prioritising your needs. The ability to put one's own needs above those of others is a life skill that should not be overlooked. People-pleasing, on the other hand, is a bad habit. Choosing between the two is entirely up to you.

Fear of love and acceptance

Another driving element behind people-pleasing habits is a sense of self-doubt and unworthiness. When you're lacking in any way, you strive to make up for it by gaining the acceptance of others. Because you feel that putting others first is the only way to obtain respect, regard, and affection from those around you, you constantly put others first. Is it possible to be a person who is only valuable to others if you can be of service to them for as long as they need or want you to be?

So, how do you correct such erroneous perceptions? It's essential to adopt a fresh perspective on oneself. Realising your intrinsic value as a person, recognising your abilities, and accepting that you do not have to be flawless to be worthy are all necessary first steps. Instead of relying on people to embrace and adore you, you'll be able to accomplish it for yourself. Building self-confidence and prioritising your own goals can help ensure that you no longer rely solely on others to feel loved and valuable.

It's particularly difficult to come to terms with your true self when you're still working on it. You can use Paul Dalton's principles for self-acceptance as a guide to help you get through this difficult time.

When you're thinking, you feel it. What you believe shapes your perception of the world and yourself. As long as you believe that the world will accept you only if you put others first, you'll see nothing but proof. To be happy, you need to believe that you can only be happy if other people like you, and if they don't like you, you'll feel unhappy.

In the mind of someone like Sofia, the only path to contentment is gaining the approval of others. So many people adore and appreciate her when she puts them first, which makes her very happy. She becomes depressed if she cannot obtain the praise of others and instead receives their condemnation. Because she believes that she can never be happy unless everyone accepts her, Sofia is unable to be content with anything less than total acceptance. What's causing her problems is her erroneous idea that happiness results from things happening to her outside of her control.

The mistake in Sofia's thinking is more obvious when stated in this manner, but it is more difficult to recognise such erroneous views in oneself. Asking yourself tough questions about your views and opinions on relationships, happiness, and yourself might help you recognise these distortions. "What am I doing to make myself happy?" is an excellent question. Also, ask yourself, "What are my core ideas about my value as a human being?" Make a point to reflect on your responses in a notebook to understand your thinking better.

Inside you'll find everything you're looking for. It's tempting to feel that everything worth having is something outside of yourself in this modern age of social media when flaunting status symbols and comparing your life to others is so easy. Dalton refers to this as the "learned self," a version of yourself that relies on external validation to feel worthy and acceptable.

On the other hand, the taught self serves to isolate you from your "unconditioned self," which is the authentic version of you that you were born with. The unconditioned self is who you are, the part of you that hasn't been influenced by any of the negative experiences you've had in your life. You are enough and worthy even if you don't have a lot of material success or external acclaim. Everything wonderful is within, and true happiness can only be found in one's soul. The only way to quit relying on the approval of others to make you feel worthy is to rediscover your true self.

Take a break, unplug, and spend time alone to rejuvenate your unconditioned self. Take a trip to a serene location where you can reconnect with your innermost self. Remember who you were before you succumbed to the pressures of society and morphed into a person you are not.

Everything in your life depends on your relationship with yourself. Everything in your life is influenced by how you feel about yourself and how you treat yourself. A self-blaming, self-berating relationship will lead you to seek the approval and affection you desire from others, but you can't offer yourself. Those who take advantage of your frantic desire for acceptance will be able to abuse and taint your connections with them in the process.

A person who thinks he or she is not deserving of love is more likely to tolerate abuse from a partner, for example. You may have been subjected to years of verbal or emotional abuse because you've treated yourself in the same harsh manner for so long. If pleasing others gives you a sense of worth and affection, you'll want to keep doing it even if others are taking advantage of you.

To break out of this vicious cycle, practice self-compassion and kindness. It's important to be a nice person for yourself. Forgive yourself for any mistakes or rejection you get from others. Remember that you're allowed to make mistakes, that you're not responsible for the happiness of others, and most crucially, that you're permitted to put your own needs ahead of those of others. In learning to forgive and love yourself first, you'll also begin to feel less of a need to seek the acceptance and affection of others. Soon, you'll come to appreciate liking yourself more than pleasing others, and you won't want to put yourself down after you've achieved permanent satisfaction.

If you're struggling with self-esteem issues, writing down a list of your positive attributes and a list of your positive accomplishments will help. As an example, you may add qualities like "creative," "focused," "excellent communicator," "resilient," and "honest" to your list of strengths. For example, in your list of accomplishments, you may include "awarded best project," "achieved year-end objectives," and "arranged an art display for a good cause." A list of your strengths and good attributes will help you see what you have that you would otherwise ignore due to your self-doubt.

If you're having difficulty coming up with items to put on those lists, ask a supportive friend or family member for assistance. To recognise your excellent traits, it's necessary to have another set of eyes to see them objectively, which might be tough if you don't feel worthy in the first place. Have a quick look at your lists in the morning to remind yourself of what you're capable of, regardless of whether others think you're great.

As a last thought, you may want to think about how your expectations may be causing you to feel insecure and self-conscious about your value. You're setting yourself up for failure if you expect to be the ideal parent, kid, sibling, friend, neighbour, and coworker at the same time, never offending anybody or disrupting any of those relationships. Because no one individual can meet everyone's needs perfectly, you'll always feel inadequate.

Changing your self-imposed standards to more realistic ones can help you stop believing that you are worthless and lacking in many areas of your life. For example, whether you're a mother, friend, or colleague, identify the roles you perform and the expectations you have for each one. As you execute your many responsibilities, let go of the need to be flawless and instead focus on what you can and can't accomplish for others around you. As a result, you'll be able to enjoy the feeling of accomplishment that comes from meeting those expectations rather than attempting to please everyone.

Is Self-Assertion bad or good?

A further reason to please others is the mistaken assumption that stating one's own needs and goals is inherently wrong, as is the case with those who bully others into getting what they want. You always go along with what other people want and never speak out for yourself. You don't want to be a person who is forceful in pushing their desires and demands on others, and you feel that expressing yourself entails that.

However, there is a flaw in this line of reasoning: it assumes that the only other option is to be an aggressive jerk. You'll have to go back and reexamine what it means to be aggressive to change your mindset. To be assertive, one must be able to express their views and defend themselves when necessary. Self-assurance and confidence without being pushy or arrogant are the goals here. Assertiveness is a positive quality, not a negative one. The ability to cultivate productive and pleasant connections with others depends on this attribute.

To be assertive, you must understand that it is not the same as being aggressive. Adversity may be worsened when someone is aggressive, yet boldness can help clear up a complex problem by not resorting to excessive force. As an example, if you believe you were unfairly rated by your supervisor, making strong claims of partiality is aggressive. Tailoring your concerns and requesting your supervisor to evaluate with you based on their assessment is the most forceful approach to handling this scenario. A lack of assertiveness may damage your relationships, but being forceful in the right way can strengthen them.

Assertiveness is a difficult skill to develop, especially for naturally inclined persons to please others. Being assertive may seem inappropriate if you are a people-pleaser because you tend to put others' needs before your own. Nevertheless, being assertive does not imply giving up on kindness and compassion. Stand up for yourself respectfully and compassionately.

The golden rule should serve as your guidance. The saying goes, "Do unto others as you would have others do unto you." This guideline should serve as your guide for balancing compassion with assertiveness. It would be preferable if someone refused to perform a favour for you because it was too much effort than if they did the favour while holding anger towards you. You'd probably prefer it if they refused you directly but in a kind and polite manner.

The same logic applies if the tables are turned. Your unwillingness to help another person may be more appreciated if you do it politely and firmly. No one wants someone performing a favour for them while harbouring hatred against them in the background. Your relationship may be at risk because you're not asserting yourself and allowing anger and hatred to build up, but you believe you're protecting it by attempting to please them despite yourself. As a result, being assertive is the greatest thing you can do for yourself, your partner, and your relationship.

Strive to find a solution that benefits both parties. For people-pleasers, it's common to feel tortured by a tension between their desires and the desires of others around them. When you put the needs of others ahead of your own, you'll soon fall into a harmful habit of self-neglect. If you want to avoid this, learn to assert yourself to find a solution that all parties can agree on. It's important to acknowledge the other person's real worries without ignoring your demands. Instead, assist the other party by making recommendations.

"I realise you need someone to cover your shift, but I'm afraid I'd be unavailable due to a previous engagement," this can be your response if a colleague asks whether you'd be willing to do so, but you have other arrangements. An assertive yet sympathetic answer to a buddy in need like this one is appropriate. You may be assertive while being a kind, caring, and decent person. You don't have to be a decent person all the time if you don't speak your mind or do what pleases others. People-pleasing behaviours may be replaced with self-assured actions that help you put yourself first when necessary when you learn to think differently about assertiveness and how to use it in your everyday life.

It's always better to just follow others, right?

People-pleasing is characterised by an unwillingness to say no to others, express one's thoughts and feelings, and establish one's desires. If you want to be liked by everyone, you'll probably just go along with what they want and never speak up for what you think is right. If you have a paralysing fear of confrontation, you may be forced into pleasing others even if you don't want to.

As a result, you choose to remain silent rather than say anything. You don't want to upset the apple cart, so you give in to everyone else's demands and desires. For people-pleasers, the fear of conflict and confrontation drives their conduct; therefore, if you want to quit being a doormat, you'll have to learn to conquer your concerns about these situations.

Exposure therapy and a **fear hierarchy** are two methods for overcoming your apprehensions about conflict and confrontation.

What exactly is exposure therapy? When you purposely put yourself in a scenario that causes you to worry and anxiety, you engage in exposure therapy. Begin by immersing yourself in the circumstances that elicit the least worry, and then advance to those that elicit the most extreme sensations of terror. To master this skill, you must be able to learn to tolerate the unpleasant emotions of fear and worry until they are no longer a source of concern.

Exposure therapy may help individuals overcome a broad range of phobias and anxieties. If you're afraid of snakes, dogs, spiders, or any other specific animal or scenario, you may want to try hypnosis (e.g., heights, elevators, crowded places). Exposure therapy is designed to assist people-pleasers in overcoming their fear of confrontation, which keeps them from declining others' requests and standing up for their rights. Exposure therapy may be used on your own to help you overcome your fear of confrontation and lessen your people-pleasing tendencies, even if you're not a professional therapist.

Experimenting with conflict and confrontation is an essential part of exposure therapy. If you're going to find yourself in a position like this, you will have to make it yourself. It's important to remember that exposure training doesn't mean that you'll start fighting anybody you come across on the street. Anything involving assertiveness is helpful for those who are deathly scared of dispute. A fear hierarchy will be built up from moderate conflict situations, which bring you the least amount of worry to more difficult confrontations, which cause you the most.

Make a list of your worst fears and organise them into a hierarchy. In that order, the fear hierarchy is a list of things that make you fearful and anxious. Essentially, it's a collection of triggers and situations that you've put together based on your personal experiences.

As an example, you may begin your list by doing something that normally doesn't cause you any stress, such as taking your time at the sales counter to pay and calculate your change. Even though it isn't a confrontation, a little tension is created between you and the next customer or the cashier. Though it's unlikely to lead to a long-term argument, the building stress you experience from taking too long to complete a task will push you.

Eventually, you may be able to approach a bully in a conflict scenario and establish yourself. A verbal conflict with another person is inevitable, and one who isn't likely to be the most candid of persons. You should try this near the conclusion of your exposures since it will put you under considerably more stress and strain than normal.

The fear hierarchy is a tiered list, beginning with the simplest activities and progressing to the most difficult ones. To begin the day by taking a long time to pay at the counter and then confronting a bully the next day would be counterproductive. As you go through a succession of more tough tasks, you'll be able to tolerate the pain that comes with disagreement more and more. Listed below is an example of a fear hierarchy, with particular confrontational situations that you may go through in sequence, ranging from the least anxiety-inducing to the most frightening. To get to the next phase, you must feel comfortable with the tension and internalise the belief that you can do these things without causing harm to yourself or the world. It's important to remember that this is only a sampling.

- Take your time memorising your credit card's passcode when you're at the counter.
- Allow a salesperson to distinguish between two comparable products and then ponder for a long time before making a purchase.
- Don't accept a salesperson's invitation to test out a new product or upgrade an existing service.
- If a colleague asks you to cover their shift, politely decline.
- Return food to a restaurant.
- Inform the host of a party that a snack was very salty.
- Request a new set of silverware each time you accidentally drop it in a restaurant's service.
- Request the return of something borrowed from a friend. Set a deadline for when you need it back.
- Arrive late for a meeting on purpose.
- Don't be afraid to say so when you don't like a coworker's concept or plan.

- Talk to an account representative about waiving the late penalties you were assessed due to a software error.
- Request that your obnoxious apartment neighbours reduce their noise.
- Dispute the findings of a performance evaluation done by your supervisor.
- If you've got a buddy who is always finding fault with everything, try talking to them and getting them to stop being so pessimistic.

Your concerns and fears may differ from the above in type, order, or both. You should modify your fear hierarchy to reflect this. Create a list based on the situations that are most important to you. Alternatively, if the above list mirrors the conflict scenarios you'd want to experiment with, you may reorder them according to the amount of fear they elicit. If you can't replicate a real-life conflict situation, you can always imagine it instead by picturing it in your mind. The greatest way to learn about real-world scenarios is to experience them.

The process of exposure therapy. It is believed that by forcing yourself to remain in the conflict scenario and feel the whole spectrum of feelings you are experiencing, whether it is discomfort or anger or worry or fear, you will be able to endure and accept those tough emotions and more. To be effective in managing conflict, you must be comfortable enough to remain with the tough feelings that it may trigger, and that can only be achieved if you stop avoiding it whenever it arises in your life. Things aren't as awful as you thought they were, and you've made it through just fine. Fears and concerns might be eased by the understanding that there will be no negative effects.

As an example, if you are exposed to the events indicated in the sample fear hierarchy above, you will experience the unpleasant sensations and scary thoughts that come with conflict. You'll be worried, humiliated, and agitated if you take a long time to recall your credit card passcode while the line of people waiting to pay increases. The world will not cease or die because of how many eyes keep piercing at you as long as you refuse to succumb to the pressure of going on.

You may be told to speed up, but that's about its extent. No, expressing dissatisfaction or speaking out against unfair treatment does not mean the end of your life as you know it. This idea applies to every phase of the process. As a result of such encounters, you gain confidence in your ability to remain calm in the face of a crisis. As you face more and more difficult situations, your tolerance for the discomfort that comes with confronting conflict and confrontation grows.

While exposing yourself to conflict situations, you may want to attempt some relaxing techniques. Deep breathing might help calm your rapid heartbeat, clammy hands, and short breaths while experiencing anxiety-inducing symptoms. Breathe in through your nose for five counts, then exhale through your pursed lips for another five counts. Do this for a total of 10 breaths. The conflict scenario triggers anxiety sensations; therefore, deliberately relaxing your breathing will conflict with them. Once you've done this, your body and mind will begin to believe that anxiety isn't as bad as you made it out to be.

The goal of exposure training is to help you understand that conflict and confrontation aren't nearly as horrible as you've previously allowed yourself to think. It's perfectly OK to decline a friend's invitation to a party, and it won't harm your friends. No harm will come from telling a salesman that you don't want to sign up for their service. Exposure therapy teaches you that you can confront others and even ignite conflict, yet you may still emerge unhurt from experience. This strategy teaches you that confronting people is acceptable when the circumstance demands it. You'll probably never be able to shake the tingling sensation you get after saying no, but it becomes simpler and easier with practice.

For eradicating people-pleasing tendencies, you must learn how to conquer your fear of disagreement and confrontation. The less fearful you are of telling others what you believe, refusing to comply with their requests, or sticking up for yourself, the more resistant you are to being coerced or bullied. You get the confidence to stand up for yourself, speak out for what you believe in, and begin making decisions that benefit your health and happiness. Because of this, you no longer have to worry about keeping your relationships exciting and gratifying for the people you care about. You get more than simply freedom from people-pleasing behaviour; you also gain the ability to stand on your own two feet.

4

Get rid of our old routines

SELF-AWARENESS IS the first habit we need to cultivate. We don't comprehend people-pleasing, and we don't even know when we're doing it. We are condemned to repeat history if we don't learn from the mistakes of the past. We can avoid the triggers and lessen the effects of our behaviour if we know what makes us do it and how it makes us feel while we're doing it.

Start by asking yourself, "Why am I doing this for them?" Do I care for them because I'm terrified of what might happen if they were gone? "Am I acting of my own free will, or am I acting on behalf of someone else?" Is there respect and connection from you, or is there fear or guilt coupled with your people-pleasing behaviours? To identify whether you are behaving out of your own free will or out of a desire to please others, going through a checklist of questions may be a simple and effective way to increase your self-awareness whenever you feel the need to please others.

It's a challenge for everyone to look at their feelings objectively. You may find it difficult to give your sentiments the respect they deserve if you're a people-pleaser who prioritises others before yourself. After all, you're putting your feelings in the trunk. So, even though it's hard, it's critical to be conscious that you're going to do something detrimental.

We learn to transform ourselves by acknowledging our realities. We can't govern our reality if we're always responding to sensations we're unaware of or in touch with.

The more you know about yourself, the easier it will be for you to figure out why you're putting in so much effort to please others. You'll be able to see whether your efforts have a positive impact or if they have a negative one. You may also notice a chance to make an alternative option before you succumb to people-pleasing.

Recognise when you're ready to embark on a joint endeavour with another person that your heart isn't quite in it. As soon as it occurs, you should halt everything and reflect on why you're doing the action in the first place. The only way to discover the truth about yourself is to keep asking, "why?" Another option is the "five whys" approach, where you ask yourself "why" five times and answer yourself to find out what's wrong with your situation.

Let's assume you and a bunch of pals often go camping. Most of the preparation work, such as erecting the tent, preparing the meals, and gathering the other goods, falls on your shoulders. You're the camp's go-to person, always looking out for the needs of others.

You're not a big fan of camping—at least, not enough to spend four weeks of the summer doing it. No one except you and your pals seemed to be having a good time. You'd rather be at home with a glass of wine and binge-watching a few episodes of your favourite show on Netflix.

"What's the point of going camping?" It's what your friends do, and you want to be friendly.

What is it about camping that makes it the only option? Because you haven't come up with another way to pass the time.

You may be asking yourself, "Why am I responsible for most of the setup when I don't even want to be?" Since you haven't expressed your need for assistance, your inclination is toward doing things on your own instead of talking about them, and so on.

From then, the possibilities are endless. The basis of your issue will be revealed at some time, and ideally, this idealistic experience will cause you to review and alter your approach to people-pleasing.

Developing self-reliance

Personal autonomy is the second habit to develop. The problem with pleasing others is that it obscures your true self. You are a puppet of someone else's power structure. It's up to others to tell you what's right and wrong. You're not allowed to express your views unless you're certain that everyone else shares your viewpoints. You have essentially vanished off the face of the earth. It may seem harsh, but it's an honest depiction of a person who is obedient to the will of others. In the absence of autonomy, it is both a habit and a deliberate decision.

We all want the approval of others. Acclaim, praises and appreciation are the fuel that keeps us going. That's OK, and it's perfectly acceptable. In contrast, people-pleasers depend on the approval of others for their happiness. They are completely reliant on the views of others since they have such a poor sense of self-worth. In the same way that they're a shadow, they're always reacting to the actions of others.

Why does this cause harm? Because, once again, it is a sham. It seems as though you've been welcomed into a squad or alliance, but in reality, you're getting more isolated. Even if you're being praised for what you've done, that's only a reflection of what you've done and not who you are. Rather than your character, traits, or abilities, you're propelled by a desire for approval—not by those things.

That's why autonomy—the capacity to think and act on one's own—is so important. Autonomous people can articulate their beliefs and the rationale behind them. They are uninhibited and certain in their actions. They can make their own decisions and don't try to avoid taking responsibility for their actions. When questioned, they don't hesitate to express their thoughts. Being self-reliant is incompatible with relying on others to thrive. To break away from others' expectations, one must believe in their power.

Autonomous people assist others because they are moved by their feelings or purposes, not those of the outside world, and this is why they do it. You decided of your own free will not to escape rejection or condemnation. Real respect is generated by self-reliant people, rather than the superficial praise and accolades that motivate people-pleasers to do the right thing.

As an example, imagine that you're working on your company's annual report alongside others. You've been given the task of writing the narrative. Your previous reports have tended to be a touch dry and uninspiring. You believe this is why no one pays attention to them once they've been published.

According to others who have worked on the report over the previous several years, the drafting has been good. The message is clear and concise, so there's no need to spend more time on it. A lack of concern for "making people care" is evident in their approach. If they tell you to stop working so hard, just follow their advice and go on with your life.

You heed the advice of others around you. Then you just disregard it. Develop methods of presenting the facts so that it is easier to comprehend. You use stories to convey your company's ideals. In your writing, you accomplish things that no one else has done before—things that no one else has ever considered. A new swivel chair is gently given to you to appreciate your effort when the report is out, and everyone takes notice.

As opposed to in the past when you would have taken the easy way out and done what everyone else was doing, you've now made a choice and are moving ahead regardless of what others think.

It's a lot simpler to talk about autonomy than it is to achieve it. You've put your viewpoint ahead of the opinions of others in the previous scenario. In any case, you respected it equally and didn't automatically devalue the views of others because you were used to doing so. When it comes to cultivating a habit of self-determination, that's where it all begins. There is a reason you're in this particular room, and you should utilise it as proof to back up your ideas.

Making fewer efforts

There must be an easier way to accomplish things. That's an interesting perspective.

People-pleasers approach all interactions with the mindset that they must go to great lengths to please others, whether personal or professional. Because of this, they are willing to go above and above to get them to do their jobs. A direct link between how much they please and how much they are praised seems to them. An enormous amount of work on their behalf is required at the very least.

The reality is that overworking and doing too much is not conducive to a healthy workplace. The more time you devote to your relationship, the less time there is for other activities in your life. Even if your intentions are good, the imbalance weakens the connection and encourages an unhealthy dynamic in which lopsidedness is expected. Assuming that one partner doing all of the heavy lifting in a relationship may compensate for the other's workload is incorrect. It's safe to say that there isn't any kind of connection if such is the case.

Successful relationships, whether they be with coworkers or a significant other, are built on mutual ownership of responsibilities and mutual support of one another. Equity and consideration are prominent themes. Attempting to fulfil the responsibilities of others while maintaining a healthy working relationship is a recipe for disaster. True to cliché, you can't respect or love anybody else if you don't first respect or love yourself, which involves recognising when you're pushing yourself too hard and taking a step back when necessary.

Fight the need to create a relationship in which one person makes all the effort and receives nothing in return, which comes from trying to satisfy others. Self-awareness is required here as well. Take an honest look at your relationship and see if there is a gap in how much each person contributes. "Would this individual do for me what I've done for them?" is a simple question to ask yourself and answer honestly.

Stop working too much after you've realised you're overworking. You'll have to draw a line in the sand at some time. It's not going to be easy, particularly given our need to "secure" our position in the hearts of others. We believe that when we're not moving, we're losing track of things and missing out on possibilities. The expression "less is more" suggests that pulling back will enable others to step forward and level the playing field. Instead of merely reacting, you must allow others the freedom to act on your behalf.

Assume you're in charge of a household's financial planning. How much money do you have available for your family's needs? They simply believe you've got it all under control because you don't say anything to the contrary. Therefore no one else in your family pays attention to the budget either.

You're the one who does all the shopping. You're the one who's in charge of getting everything done. You're in charge of everyone's phone and internet service. You decide on the computer and technology requirements and provide funds appropriately. In the midst of all this, your kids are whining that you didn't bring them the beverages they wanted or that their internet connection is too sluggish for their online games.

Think of it this way: "Forget it," you tell yourself. "I can no longer make all these choices on my own." People will have to make certain choices if they want anything. In addition, it wouldn't hurt if they helped out with part of the shopping." You decide to cut down on what you're currently doing.

So you instruct the children to write down everything they need or want. It's up to them to figure it out. Your spouse knows you'd prefer it if they did some of the buying, particularly for items specific to their desires. You instruct everyone to keep an eye on their personal mobile data use. They'll perform a domestic duty while you're gone to the store since you can't do it yourself. Was it that tough, other than that you had to realise you had to do it?

You've reduced your workload, delegated responsibilities, and removed yourself from the "people-pleasing" circuit by making others take responsibility for their own needs. It isn't easy to adopt the practice of doing less and delegating and/or relaxing since, once again, it seems like things are slipping away from us. They aren't. If you don't do anything, it doesn't imply that someone else isn't taking care of things.

Developing the ability to let go

It is an unfortunate fact of life that some people do and say horrible things. Their deeds and words might haunt them for a long time, or perhaps forever, for the unlucky individuals who are the victims of their actions and words. Bullies and doomsayers have been around for a long time, and many of them go unpunished. The destructive nature of some is even venerated.

To relate or even comprehend such pessimistic individuals is a waste of time. In the end, it's irrelevant; they've already happened. Our memories of what they've done to us are often haunted by what they've done to us. No matter how hard we try, we can't shake the dreadful feelings that their harsh deeds and poor views have left us with. In the present, we let our past experiences influence our ideas and prevent us from pursuing our dreams. It's important to remember that your previous experiences don't reflect your life now; therefore, don't let them affect you negatively. You can't rely on your emotions or recollections to tell you what's genuine.

Of course, it's easier said than done to put those upsetting recollections in your mind. Negative remarks can't be ignored. It's not simple to get rid of the crap they've implanted in you. Even still, our refusal to break free of the shackles of the past prevents us from moving forward. We cling to their criticism like a prized possession. Thus, we constantly fear an unseen rebuke, which causes us to scramble to satisfy everyone.

The issue isn't addressed in this manner. The situation controls our minds, and we aren't able to learn from it. We are not our pasts as products of our history, particularly the portions we didn't want to be part of. We are who we are now because we deliberately decided to be that way.

In the first place, we want to get rid of the issue, but it doesn't imply we've solved it. As a result, we do not want to deal with any emotional suffering that the situation may create, nor do we want any unpleasant consequences that may arise. Instead of dealing with the issue, we simply avoid it and hope it goes away. You know it will not go away, so don't waste your time.

Because of this, if we have a flashback to someone else's pain, we flee in terror and do whatever it takes to make the present circumstance seem right. People-pleasing conduct follows.

For example, let's assume you live with a roommate you perform most of your chores for. They are not idle or irresponsible, but you constantly place yourself in the position of cooking for them, doing their clothes, etc. Despite their apparent discomfort, they offer to help, but you insist on carrying on nonetheless.

Why? As a result of being bullied as a youngster for being sluggish, never doing anything right, or always falling short, you've carried those scars into adulthood. To counter this, you've decided to become a servant.

We can make these conditions acceptable in a true sense by letting go of the past. It's up to you to decide to do so, though. Another important step is to recognise and not attempt to avoid or dismiss the grief that the previous incident has given you. As painful or unimaginable as it may be, reclaiming your power from the previous bullies is a need. They've gone, but you remain. I'm not saying that you have to forgive them, but it's a good idea to do so in many circumstances. Most of us are just doing the best we can with the available resources, and we have no desire to harm anybody or anything in our path.

You'll find yourself more self-confident and free to be who you are after you've dealt with your past and learned to let it go.

Honesty is a virtue

Disguising oneself is an essential part of people-pleasing. You're encasing yourself in the service of others, obscuring your own identity. Your genuine sentiments, ideas and views are hidden in this kind of dishonesty. Even if you don't want to admit it, suppressing your emotions is usually always a bad idea in the long run.

As a result, you must develop the practice of speaking your mind openly. For others to understand where you stand, you need to be more open and honest with them. It's unrealistic to expect others to know what you want since they can't read minds. Indicate clearly and unequivocally what you need or want, believing that this is what you are entitled to. To put it another way, it's like being less filtered or more honest with yourself.

Regardless of the circumstances, it is evident that you are dishonest with daily individuals you interact with.

Consequently, there may be some moderate tension or strain in expressing a viewpoint that others may disagree with. You must allow yourself to anticipate and learn to accept this feeling of unease.

Let's assume you spend every day with a group of buddies. Most of your time is spent in bars, where you consume far too much alcohol. Drinking appears to be an important part of the group's identity, and you like being a part of it. Your physical and emotional health may be suffering, and you may notice that the group bond is weakening. So far, you have avoided saying anything because you are afraid of losing the friendship of your buddies.

You haven't had to make any major changes until now, but now you've reached a point where you have to. To obtain help, you message the group and tell them that you're scared and worried about becoming chemically addicted and that you need to concentrate on getting well. Perhaps a group exercise in the great outdoors would be ideal for them all.

The desire to be liked by others is a fundamental driver of people-pleasing behaviour. But here's the thing: doing what you want to do doesn't need the approval of others. Do anything you want if you aren't aiming to commit a crime or do something harmful to yourself or others. Saying you're going to do something is better than saying you're thinking about it and then asking if it's acceptable. It's time to act.

It's common for people-pleasers to wonder whether or not they deserve the things they seek. Because they've been putting the needs of others ahead of their own, how can they know whether they deserve what they want?

That's a simple yes or no question, and the unanimous response is yes. Instead of getting caught up in the never-ending loop of desiring something and then second-guessing whether you deserve it, concentrate on what you need. If you don't try, you won't get what you want 100% of the time—but that's better than having no chance.

Setting personal limits is an important part of this process, and we'll go into that in more detail in the following chapter. When you're a people-pleaser, you don't dare set boundaries for others to follow. Because they don't know your boundaries, even those who don't want to take advantage of you may do so because they don't know what they are. Defining your limits with clear clarity goes a long way toward preventing future disagreements and mishaps. To help you recover the part of yourself that blindly pleasing other people takes away.

Making such a request might make you feel quite uneasy. A little more convincing may be required if you're not sure you're eligible. In situations like these, it's a good idea to take notes.

Make a note of why you're requesting something before bringing it up in your appeal. It's important to be thorough and honest. Focus on your logic and get a thorough understanding of it since this will be the most important component of your bargaining technique when you make your request.

You don't need to break out PowerPoint and construct an elaborate presentation with charts and figures if all you're asking is for someone to perform a favour for you. Writing down your ideas might help you organise your thoughts, even if the request is modest. And if you'd like, you can go over your notes with a trusted friend or family member. If you're having a hard time justifying this request, then it may not be reasonable in the first place.

Strengthening yourself when things get tough

Disapproval, the sworn adversary of every people-pleaser ever, awaits you once you decide to be more assertive. Some vocal criticism or outspoken disagreement may be necessary. No doubt some of them will sting. However, they aren't going to harm you.

The most difficult element of your journey away from people-pleasing conduct may be dealing with this sort of censure. This is also the one that may yield the highest dividends since it will help you deal with any kind of problem, even ones that are more serious than a fight.

Consider the cause of your complaint before moving on to other issues. If your detractors are concerned about you, they may not be concerned about you at all—they may be concerned about themselves. Thoughtful consideration should be given to whether or not their criticisms are meant to fix your "mistake." They may be criticising you because they are expressing and projecting their concerns. Alternatively, they may not understand what it's like to be in your position or have any clue of what's going on in your world. It's OK to provide constructive criticism, but the giver's perspective often taints it. The more they exert pressure on you, the more serious the problem becomes. Consider the likelihood of such a scenario.

A quick response is nearly always unnecessary when you're in front of the person making the judgment. Take a few deep breaths to calm yourself down when someone criticises you or moans about how you do things.

Also, consider that you do not have to react at all. You're under no responsibility to respond to your critics' negativity if you don't want to. You may simply disregard them and continue on your way. This isn't good in every case—you surely don't want to ignore the ideas of your spouse or a police officer, but it's OK in arguments that don't matter that much in the long run.

However, if you want to participate in the back and forth, remember what we discussed in the previous section: disputes are OK. It's usual for two individuals to disagree on the same topic. It's not uncommon for those two individuals to go on to have fruitful and enjoyable relationships following their argument.

In all cases, when you're dealing with someone furious with you, don't automatically assume that you're the one in the wrong. People-pleasers often accept that quick judgment to keep the peace, but it's not always correct. To win back someone's favour, you may be more willing to compromise your principles if you can't bear the thought of them being angry with you. Consider the context in which your critic is making their argument. Depending on the person's response, it might reveal more information about them than you.

People-pleasers, on the other hand, are more likely to agree. As soon as someone tells them what to do, they do it right away. That said, it's wise to avoid the temptation to agree at the moment. The recovering people-pleaser may experience some small anguish due to this, since withholding an immediate reaction will put emotional pressure on their system. Pressure will never be more intense or tough than it was the first time you resisted succumbing to it. To resist the temptation to succumb to pressure, you just need five seconds of great willpower. Even if you keep seeing the same individual, it becomes less of a challenge.

But remember, you have the right to do anything you want. This means postponing your answer, whether it's for just a few minutes or a few days. You're doing the right thing by delaying your response until you've had time to consider it. Most importantly, focus on what's most important to you.

Do not feel responsible for how other people feel

Finally, make it a practice to know precisely what you are and are not accountable for.

It's not uncommon for the people-pleaser to assume a great deal of responsibility for the well-being of others, even in circumstances that don't include them. We take responsibility for our actions if we make someone feel awful due to our increased assertiveness or sense of self.

You have an innate drive to protect other people's emotional well-being, yet this impulse also makes you unhappy.

Consequently, if your assertiveness causes a negative or strong reaction from someone, the people-pleaser will quickly see it as their responsibility to rectify or avoid the situation. In other words, this isn't an issue of giving but rather about obtaining acceptance and eliminating insecurity. Your unconscious belief that you are in control of how others feel and cope with their emotions and overall happiness is reinforced by your habitual behaviour.

Nothing could be farther from the truth than holding a kid responsible for their parents' fights or holding a spouse accountable for their partner's employment problems. However, it happens frequently. Regardless of the circumstances, we take action to alleviate our erroneous guilt.

You need to take a hard look at who you're accountable for and what you can do about it. If you expect others to bear so much of the burden, you're setting yourself up for failure. It's not true that you have that huge a duty; it's all in your head.

Many moving pieces and billions of people/animals make up

the globe, which is always in change. There are many variables for one individual to manage to take care of for everyone else's emotions.

Take a moment to reflect on your circumstances. Everything in life is based on random factors, many of which we have no power to influence. When making a choice, you usually consider a variety of elements, such as the circumstance you've been placed in, the impact of people near to you, and so on. To go where you want to go in life, you have to rely on many external factors. Everyone else does the same. You can't be held responsible for everything.

Instead of blaming others, take responsibility for your actions and outcomes. What you think, say and do are all examples of this. Emotions are the responsibility of the individual, not the collective. And they are the only ones who can control their feelings. Being less empathic toward other people while being more compassionate toward oneself is an important habit to cultivate.

As a result, you may believe that making others happy is a virtue or that it makes you a better human being. However, this is not the case. The noblest thing to do is give up your happiness and health to make others happy. It's self-serving. Whenever you pay attention to someone who continually blames themselves, you're teaching them to be self-deprecating. In addition, you're teaching children to rely on you. Helping those who don't need it is a way for many individuals to feel good about themselves. Even though these folks have no notion of who they are, they realise that others need them. At the very least, that's what they're telling themselves.

People-pleasers are not born—they're made. To keep their home from falling, they've been conditioned by the behaviours they've adopted and left untreated. Changes in attitude and thinking may go a long way toward eliminating harmful habits, creating new ones, and eventually obtaining emotional liberation for oneself and others.

5

Set your limits

TO CEASE PEOPLE-PLEASING, you need to set limits. We often don't even know that we're giving someone complete access to our personal space and allowing them to invade it. People-pleasing habits are exacerbated when we let ourselves be taken over by others.

Some boundaries apply to you and the individuals you interact with. There is no way we can work well if we don't limit our conduct and habits. Some examples of self-imposed boundaries include:

- Restricting the amount of time you spend on a single task.
- Establishing a spending limit to prevent yourself from overspending on unnecessary items.
- Watching what you eat and drink.
- Establishing annual goals that are both reasonable and attainable.
- Maintaining a routine that does not overburden you with your job or social obligations.

What hope do you have that you will be able to provide for

everyone else if you can't provide for yourself? It's usually a good idea to start by identifying your limits when trying to live ethically and pleasantly. However, a healing people-pleaser must set clear limits with those around him or her.

What makes a boundary?

A boundary is an unnoticeable wall that separates your personal space from the area of others. Emotional space is included in this concept, and physical space (the immediate, literal region surrounding you). We're more interested in the emotional side of making people happy.

To keep others from trespassing on your personal space, you need to set boundaries for yourself. They regulate your "space" to be who you are without the interference of other people. To avoid being overly dependent on people or enmeshed in another persona, you'll need this room to keep a safe distance. In addition, a good boundary helps you avoid becoming completely isolated or aloof.

As soon as you establish clear boundaries, you feel freer to express yourself without the pressure of others' expectations or demands. This gives you the freedom to express yourself more freely and independently, allowing you to stand out more from the crowd. This buffer zone permits you to think more calmly and easily about specific scenarios. As long as you've established your boundaries based on your requirements, a reasonable boundary allows you to invite anybody you want to share your emotions with.

For people-pleasers, establishing limits and making sure others are happy is more important than finding their pleasure. They either don't know about or grossly underestimate the importance of setting these boundaries. Making clear limits and putting your foot down is critical to breaking the "people-pleasing" cycle.

When to set boundaries and how to recognise when it's time

It might be tough to recognise when others are invading our personal space and exceeding our limitations when one is caught up in people-pleasing. After all, you've portrayed yourself as always there for others, regardless of their own needs. Other people's responsibilities fall within your purview. What's the point of continuing? Understanding what it feels like to cross a healthy boundary is the first step in establishing healthy boundaries.

You must pay attention to your body and mind to do so. How does your body react when you're around someone who's bothering or exhausting you? You may notice a tightness of your stomach or tenseness in your brain as common symptoms. Also, describe how you feel when you're around this person—do you feel confused, inattentive, or racing with ideas on how to escape? Boundaries that have been crossed may go undetected at the time, but the consequences will be obvious. After a conversation, you'll know how tense or uncomfortable you are.

You'll have some time to figure out just what it is about this person that annoys you after that diagnosis. Abrasiveness, hyperactivity, and inattention to detail: are these traits inherent in the person? Are they too direct for your taste? Do they say things to upset or irritate you? Remember that you don't have to reveal this knowledge to anybody else, so be open and honest with yourself.

You've created a kind of alarm system using the information you've gathered—your physical reaction, mental reaction, and the problem with the individual. In the future, if you've followed these procedures to the letter, you'll be able to recognise any of these behaviours as signs that you need to reevaluate or set boundaries.

Your personal and emotional space will be invaded if someone begins to place things in it that aren't yours. It's a common misconception that boundaries can only be violated specifically, such as barging into your home and demanding tea. Still, in truth, any time you feel uncomfortable, someone has likely violated a boundary. Keep in mind that you have a stake in this.

As an illustration, consider the following. They are sisters, Eva and Elena. Elena had just finished introducing her family to her new boyfriend, Luca. A few months after Luca started showing up at family gatherings, Eva spent more time with him.

When Eva was around Luca, however, everything went awry. When Luca asked her a question, it troubled her stomach. Her thoughts became jumbled. Because of her fear, she had the want to leave. But she didn't want to reprimand Luca in front of Elena, fearing an altercation in the household.

When Eva reflected on her reactions to Luca's presence, she discovered that he seemed unusually preoccupied with other people's private lives, particularly the romantic ones. Luca was unusually open in their chats and asked intimate questions that bordered on intrusiveness. A nice tone pervaded the exchange as though this were a normal part of every family's daily routine. He had no idea his questions were raising a few eyebrows. But Eva, a very private person, was pushed to the limit by them. Eva's assessment of the situation prompted her to put certain boundaries.

The following time Luca and Eva got together, he immediately discussed Eva's online dating experiences. After Elena heard Eva tell her that she'd sworn off online dating for good, she must have told Luca. "I've been thinking about this for a long time, and I simply don't feel comfortable discussing my personal life in that much depth," Eva told Luca. "I appreciate your politeness, but I ask that you respect my boundaries in this regard."

Astonished, Luca was shocked. No, he didn't know what he was doing when he asked those questions. He walked away with a murmured apology. Eva never heard from him again. There was a period of around eight months after the conflict when Elena and Luca continued to date. Eva and Luca never had a romantic relationship, but they did maintain a cordial and amicable relationship up until their breakup, after which Eva lost contact with him completely.

Everything turned out well for Eva in the end. In a worst-case scenario, Elena would have been distraught, Luca would have been enraged, and the family would have been broken. But regardless of the outcome, Eva was correct in stating that she had to establish a barrier.

In some cases, creating boundaries might lead to repercussions, especially for individuals who are naïve rather than malicious. However, the consequences are almost always worth it, as Eva demonstrated. It may be tough to discern the truth when emotions are running high, yet it's not even close.

How to create boundaries in your life

Hopefully, you've improved your self-awareness to the point where you know it's time to assert your right to privacy. Now is the moment to do a thorough self-examination and establish clear boundaries that will aid you in overcoming your need to please others. Here are a few steps to get you started.

What is it that truly matters to you? The pace of daily life might make it difficult to recognise who you are and what matters to you. Even if we have the time, some of us never engage in such self-examination. Some of us may simply think about what other people tell us to believe or value, such as our religious views, cultures, and traditions.

Consider what you value most and what makes up your own unique personal code before putting all of that to one side. Think about what makes you uncomfortable and how it affects your behaviour to get an idea of this. Don't worry about them being big or noteworthy; they don't have to be. You may not even notice them if they happen frequently enough.

Hugo, for example, could not bear the thought of paying an astronomical amount for a parking space. As a result, he rejects it (or, probably more to the point, what he could afford). But he lived in a huge city, where parking at professional sporting events often cost more than $100 for six hours, so he couldn't afford it. Hugo has no intention of dealing with such an issue. Instead, he parked his car at a park-and-ride and rode the $5 round-trip light rail to the game.

A stunning tale, I know. Hugo's ideas may be gleaned even from a brief story like this one:

- He's cheap, at least when it comes to parking.

- He has no problem going "the long way" if necessary.

- He believes in the use of public transportation.

What I mean by "surface values" is a series of indicators as to what Hugo's core values might be. Using a little decryption, we can identify some of Hugo's key values:

- Financial accountability.
- Patience.
- Public-mindedness.

Try this mental exercise using some of the things you perform regularly. Consider how you act in a given scenario, habit, or event, and see if you can connect it to any core beliefs you hold. The values you discover may be something you weren't aware of before. As many instances as you can come up with, you'll notice that a few basic principles will keep cropping up more frequently than others, and those are probably the ones you truly believe in.

Keeping in mind your beliefs and what makes you feel comfortable or uneasy is essential while examining an incident that involves a relationship with another person. Rather than focusing on what the other person might value or framing your values in terms of your connection with them, focus on what you value. This practice requires a certain amount of self-indulgence on your part because you're attempting to identify what it is that you desire. It's okay to be self-obsessed during this operation. You'll be more resolute and less inclined to appease others if you have a clearer sense of what you believe in.

Only you can make a difference in your life. You might believe, "This scenario would be better if my friends/partners/parents/children/coworkers would accept my way of thinking. There would be no issue if everyone could see things my way."

It's natural to desire that. You can't help but tell everyone how you fixed yourself once you find a solution: "I was messed up! I'm back to normal now! Unfortunately, you haven't changed at all. Make sure you follow this example."

There's the possibility that we're just tired of individuals being so difficult to deal with. They should cease being lazy around the house, their bosses shouldn't criticise them, and their pals shouldn't go overboard. That's understandable.

Go back to our last chapter's advice on overcoming bad habits:

"Assume and express your self-resilience, the things you can fully control."

We are not liable for the actions of other people. Furthermore, attempting to change the behaviour of others has a very low success rate. The only thing you can and should do is change your relationship with others. You can't stop people from trying to cross your boundaries, but you can adjust how you respond when they do.

This does not imply that you must accommodate them (a people-pleaser move). Change your strategy by the values we've just found and operate in a way that signals boundaries. It requires rethinking how you interact with people who are causing you problems. When someone is extremely aggressive in using your personal space, you need to emotionally stake your position.

Consider the case of a close friend who has a problem with excessive spending. They're constantly stocking up on unnecessary items. These people have a lot of possessions and take vacations frequently, despite being broke.

You know they'd change their ways if they merely had stricter budgetary methods. Just like you, they may benefit from paying more attention to their bank accounts and developing better financial strategies. Not at all. This person's issues aren't your fault. Fixing them would take too much time away from your work. The things you're dealing with are your own business. But the only thing you can do is stop handing them money. You can only adjust your behaviour such that it doesn't enable or promote the actions of others. Someone else's mental model of the world does not include you.

Rather than persuading others to change their minds, it's better to change your behaviour. It's much more productive and fruitful for your health if you can work independently and make changes for yourself.

Decide what will happen. So what happens once someone trespasses into your personal space despite you telling them to respect your boundaries?

It's entirely up to you, really within the bounds of reason. Neither starting a street fight nor hacking into their computer is acceptable behaviour. However, you have the right to stand up for yourself emotionally and protect your own space. You must decide what will happen if someone crosses your line to do this. If you want to do nothing at all, you can.

What if someone on Facebook keeps bugging you about a disagreement they are involved in? When he continues to bother you in public, despite your warnings, it's clear he doesn't get the message. As a result, you have the option of either unfriending or blocking him from future contact on Facebook.

You may find this part emotionally challenging. It's a nerve-wracking time. Then, it's a part of establishing your limits. Regardless of what everyone else thinks, this is solely for your benefit. That is what you have to do. There comes the point when you have to step in if someone keeps crossing that threshold despite your repeated pleas to stop.

Of course, you might expect a negative response from them. Judgmental, short-sighted or unfair are just some of the labels you could get from others who don't understand your perspective. Expect them to behave in this manner. Assume it's a part of determining the punishment. However, don't let it influence your decision.

It's also a good idea to write down the implications of your actions in advance. It's always a good idea to jot down notes, but it's extremely prudent in this case. Make a list of your boundaries, the behaviours that might cross those boundaries, and the repercussions you expect if those boundaries are crossed. Writing helps you keep track of your thoughts and might serve as a helpful reminder if you ever need to go back to what you've chosen. Emotional or frightening situations can make it harder to make sensible decisions, but understanding what we've already determined with an open mind might help us act.

People-pleasers are so afraid of being disliked that they allow offences against them to go unresolved. You'll gain more self-control and self-respect if you have a clear policy regarding the repercussions of going above your boundaries.

Setting boundaries: A few more steps

You're the only one who knows what's most important to you. It is only you who has the authority to create your boundaries. Although it may seem like a daunting task at first, it will give you the confidence to take the lead in reinforcing your principles. Those are essential abilities for everyone who wants to break free from a life of pleasing others.

Here are a few more methods for establishing boundaries that you might find useful.

Define your boundaries, then stick to them. What works for you and what doesn't is entirely up to you. You must be as explicit and direct as possible while establishing and defining your boundaries. No one will respect your boundaries if you don't state them clearly yourself. Those that come to your house to eat at your dining room table and leave a mess have no way of knowing that you dislike it when people do so.

Think about these boundaries in broad strokes when defining them. Determine what you desire in specific areas by using your basic values as a guide. It's important to recognise that you have a wide range of options for establishing your rules, including your personal space, personal information, money and assets, etc.

You're entitled to set different boundaries with different people in your life. Depending on how close you are to a person, you may be subject to different rules and restrictions. A family member or close friend may ask to borrow your car, but a casual acquaintance from work or the bar is completely different. It's up to you whether or not you want to change the boundaries for certain people and not for others.

Finally, folks may not understand why you've imposed certain restrictions, regulations, or boundaries on yourself. Nothing to be ashamed of there. None of this is required of them at all. You get to make those choices. What important is that your rules are understood by others, even if they don't agree with them. Don't give a fuck about it.

Make it clear to others what your boundaries are. Everybody needs to be crystal clear about the limitations you set for yourself (especially if those limits range from person to person). You owe it to yourself and others to be open, honest, and frank when setting and enforcing boundaries. You can't just assume that they'll get it right.

People keep falling asleep on your couch, for example. Someone you know always stays out late and refuses to drive back to their house on the weekends for various reasons. In other words, they come on your door, ask if they can crash, and you let them in. Within 15 minutes, your sofa is closed for the night. Then there's the possibility of them stealing food from your fridge when you're asleep. It robs you of your personal space and sucks up some of your time.

You probably haven't made it apparent that this arrangement is no longer working for you, and you should do so. Because you'd rather passive-aggressively imply that you're annoyed and would like not to have this happen, you have not explicitly established this barrier. As a result, they won't stop doing it because they aren't aware of your displeasure. As long as you don't explicitly define your boundaries, people will keep walking right over them.

Even if you only hint at it, certain individuals will pick it up. Think of the story of Eva and Luca, the guy who questioned her too much about her personal life. Why do you ask?" may have been Eva's way of indicating her boundaries. Many people will see that as a warning and back off, respecting your personal space.

Others may not be as intuitive as you are, and if they continue to ignore your signals, it's time to be more straightforward with them. This is the most difficult phase of the process. "I don't like to talk that," "I'm not going to do that," or "Please quit harping on me about this topic" could have been Eva's responses. The word "no" is a powerful tool for defending your limits. Similarly, you can say, "This is the only time you'll be able to do this without X," or simply, "This isn't going to happen again" to justify your couch.

There is no need on your part to explain to someone who does not comprehend your set of limits why you have them in place. There's no need for an explanation from you. That decision doesn't necessitate an explanation of why you made it. A thing doesn't need to be justified. You know who you are and what matters most to you. You understand why you feel this way. Everything else is a non-issue. You're not required to create a diagram for anyone else's benefit. Consider the word "no" as a whole phrase when setting boundaries.

Don't allow anyone off the hook for crossing the line. You've come to terms with what's acceptable and what's not. You've explained them to others clearly and concisely. You've outlined the consequences of your actions. Someone is still going above and beyond your boundaries. What's next?

Lay down the law and don't allow anyone to get away with breaking it—time to get moving.

When you seek to define your boundaries and demonstrate your authority, you need to put your boundaries in place. As a result, you should only make rules that you can keep. If you just intend to implement half of a restriction, you should probably rethink it. Either you don't think the limit is important or haven't worked out all the details yet. A lack of respect for your limits will be noticed and taken to indicate that you aren't taking them seriously. It's called a "blurred barrier," indicating a vulnerability that others will take advantage of right away.

Some people will take offence at your insistence on enforcing boundaries and handing out punishments. Just know that bad things will happen, and we'll go into more depth on how to deal with them in a moment.

It would have been simple, for example, to avoid being bugged by your Facebook bully friend. You could have ignored him or found a different way to deal with him if you so desired. He'll keep doing what he's doing if you enable him to have access to you. Despite your best efforts, he has ignored your explanations and boundaries. Don't look back after hitting the "unfriend" button on that social media platform.

Trying to please others is difficult for the people-pleaser, and it's even more difficult for them to stand up for themselves and face the repercussions of their actions. There will be a lot less worry in the actual action if you back up your boundaries with strong action than if you let it fester.

Resolving conflicts by determining boundaries

It's usually a good idea to plan things out ahead of time. There are times when your boundaries will be broken, and you'll have to make on-the-spot modifications to keep yourself safe and sound. To keep your boundaries intact, you'll need to respond to unexpected events in a way that is consistent with your values.

Your reaction must convey a clear message. It may be simpler to be subtle and forceful if you're trying to break your people-pleasing tendency. Being strong and determined could be impossible for you if you are used to pleasing everyone.

Some subjects and emotions that may come up unexpectedly are listed below for your reference. The first is delicate and courteous in the hopes that cues would be picked up, and then the second is direct and to the point after it becomes evident force is required. I'll give you both possible responses. Of course, this wording can be used in many situations.

MONEY: Everyone must be compensated, but there may be a few friends or associates who keep asking for more money. 'No one can expect you to continue giving away money you've earned or is legally yours to someone who doesn't respect your boundaries.'

Subtle: "I'm sorry for what's happened to you. I'm sorry, but I'm at a point in my life where I can't lend money."

Direct: "I'm sorry, but I cannot keep loaning you money. As a personal necessity, I must use it. Taking care of oneself and earning money are two things you must learn to do independently."

EXTRA RESPONSIBILITIES: We often give too much of our time away, especially when we're putting all of our efforts into something we truly care about. This is especially problematic. To avoid over-promising, you should instead protect and safeguard your time to focus on other elements of your life.

Subtle: "As much as I'd like to give my support, I'm afraid I'm already over my allotment of time. Whenever I have more time, I'd be pleased to discuss it."

Direct: "There is no way that I can be of assistance at this time. "I simply don't have the time."

COMPLAINTS THAT AREN'T HELPFUL: It's difficult to defend yourself after being shocked and injured by judgment, character assassination, or harsh remarks about your appearance or style. But it's essential to speak up as soon as possible.

Subtle: "I realise you may have been making a joke or weren't being serious, but I felt wounded at the words you said."

Direct: "I don't find your comments very amicable. If you continue to make them, I won't participate in this discussion."

ANGER: Even while disagreements are inevitable, it is all too simple for someone to cross the line into hostility and abuse when their emotions get better. You must maintain a calm but tenacious demeanour when attempting to bring the temperature down.

Subtle: "I need you to try and be less furious," says the voice in my head. "You're interfering with my ability to express myself." Reasonableness is the only path to a solution in this case. What if you tried speaking with a more measured voice?

Direct: "Don't yell at me. Please. Is it something you'd be able to live with? I'm going to leave now. As soon as you've calmed down and are no longer threatening me, we can get back to discussing this issue."

TIME IS MONEY: There may come a time when someone tells you that they urgently require you to make a decision and act immediately. "Their emergency is not your priority," says the corporate cliché. Maintain your commitment to the timetable you've set for yourself.

Subtle: "I get what you're saying. I just need some time to ponder the best course of action. Although I understand your sense of urgency, may I have a moment to return your call? That will help."

Direct: "I'm not going to force myself to make a rapid decision without more consideration. It's something I'd want to think about for a while. You have one more minute to wait for my answer, so the answer is no."

It is simpler to resist the impulse to please others if you know how to adapt and respond in the middle of an unanticipated boundary-crossing occurrence.

Consider the consequences

Now it's time to have some fun! After finally taking the initiative to respect yourself, you may find that a few others are out of shape when you do so. They will not be pleased. They'll be hurt and perhaps even depressed. Some of them may be quite angry. However, it is better to stick to your beliefs and keep your boundaries in place in the long run.

You'll grow increasingly enraged with someone if their response causes you to lower your defences. There is no way you can let them get the better of you. You need to be in a place where your friends, family, and acquaintances truly admire and appreciate you for who you are, even if they initially find your decision disappointing or upsetting.

If you want to make your boundary settings more likely to work, you have to consider some degree of risk. Allow for the possibility that someone will become enraged when you set your limits.

When dealing with someone who may be irrationally angry with you, you must strengthen your resolve. You're not going to put up with their harassment or their attempts to push you past your breaking point. You must not allow them to continue to take advantage of your good nature or helpfulness or to demonstrate contempt for the boundaries you have set for yourself.

Your situation will not improve if you allow your determination to be weakened by fear of an angry individual. This must be realised as soon as possible. If you back down from your demand that others respect your boundaries, you'll make things worse for yourself. That eventually grows into a full-blown hatred and anger.

You may feel some discomfort, but it will only last for a short time if you hold steady in the face of criticism. Even if they remain resentful for a while, you'll be satisfied knowing that you stood your ground and spoke up for what's important to you. At the very least, you'll believe that you've made the correct decision. There's a good chance their rage will subside, allowing you to rebuild your friendship.

It's not your fault they're so enraged; it's theirs. Again, you are solely accountable for your conduct. Individuals are alone in charge of how they choose to respond to the world. If you maintain a calm demeanour and stick to your beliefs about boundaries, perhaps they'll finally understand that they need to treat people with more respect.

Angry people will try to get you into trouble, but don't fall for it. Maintain your composure if their wrath begins to spiral out of control. Just because they're enraged doesn't give them the right to set the tone of the conversation. Remaining silent is a sign of strength in this situation. Allow them to have a fit and calmly get on with your day.

People-pleasers generally try to make an angry person feel better and get back into their good graces as soon as possible. They often do this without even thinking of the consequences. In other words, fight the temptation to fix everything since you'll be handing over your power to someone who will simply destroy it.

Even when you're dealing with someone enraged by your actions, such as those in which you set boundaries, the best course of action is to do nothing. The best approach isn't always the easiest, but it's the most common.

People-pleasing mindset can be broken by understanding the necessity of setting boundaries, determining one's ones, guarding against crossing them, and being forceful in defending them when they are violated. You'll be reminded of your value and beliefs if you use your strength of character to resist the temptation to please everyone.

6

Know when to say no

SAYING NO IS one of the most powerful tools in one's arsenal for self-expression. As we've seen throughout this book, it's not always our fault when we try to satisfy others. The inability to say no may not even be a deliberate choice.

Many of us have realised that the negativity and potential for conflict or disappointment we carry into a conversation is a part of ourselves. Alternatively, we don't have proper and tight boundaries to guide us. Or for any of the countless other reasons we've discussed in this book for lack of self-confidence. This chapter attempts to help you understand why saying yes when you want to say no has the same effect, no matter how many times you've done it. Even if you don't know what to do, you already have a good idea of what's going on in your head.

That doesn't instantly make saying no and removing the inherent tension easier and more comfortable. Because the tension will always be a part of your life, you may at least become more adept at saying no in ways that convey your message more quickly and effectively.

"I'm unable to" versus "I'm unwilling to"

The way we talk to ourselves affects our ability to say no, which is something you would not expect. 120 students were divided into two groups: the "I can't" group and the "I don't" group, according to a study published in the Journal of Consumer Research in 2012. When confronted with temptation, one group was instructed to say, "I can't do X," repeatedly. "I'm allergic to chocolate," for example, might be their response if they were tempted. "I don't do X" or "I don't eat chocolate" were the instructions given to the "I don't" group.

This study's findings indicated how even a small change in terminology could significantly impact our ability to say no, resist temptation, and encourage behaviour focused on achieving a goal. The "I don't" group outperformed the "I can't do" group when saying no.

Simply stating that you cannot do anything is a reminder of the constraints you have placed on your ability to achieve your goals. As a result, you're reinforcing in your mind the idea that you're unable to accomplish something you'd typically like to. When you say "I can't," you're engaging in self-discipline that you don't want to do all the time.

When you tell yourself, "I don't," you're generating a feedback loop that reminds you of your power and influence over the circumstance. You've drawn a line in the sand and now have no control over the situation. You've already decided to say no, so it's easier for you to stick to your decision. We can modify our behaviour just by altering one word in our self-talk. The word "don't" conveys a stricter answer than "can't," which encourages people to try to persuade and entice you into doing something.

For example, think of a circumstance where someone who is on a diet is given an unhealthy dessert. Using the phrase, "I can't," is a way to remind them of the restrictions imposed by their diet. They've given it some thought and have formally decided to decline. "I don't" is a better response than "I can't" because it allows them to take control of the situation and stick to their predetermined conclusion. As a reminder, they won't be eating any junk food.

Abandoning categorisation

People frequently asked for favours or duties should learn how to say no using the "I don't" concept. Consider denying the entire category rather than going through each request.

For example, instead of deciding whether or not you can or cannot accommodate each request, you'll find it far more empowered to say, "Sorry, I don't do those kinds of meetings anymore."

As a result of this method, you'll find it much easier than before to say no to requests from other people. If there's something you truly want or need to do, you can make an exception to requests. However, you'll find that opting into a request is far easier. Refusing to participate in an entire category, like declaring "I don't" instead of "I can't," is a barrier most people are willing to accept. As soon as they realise that you are a frequent exception-maker, they will try to convince you to let them be the next one.

To give you an idea of how popular Jude's crime novels have become, we'll use him as an example. As a result, he receives many requests from organisations wanting him to speak about these works at their gatherings. Jude has devised his criterion for speaking to groups about his novels after receiving inquiries from organisations as small as five or six individuals and as large as 200 people. From May through August, he won't talk to groups of less than 20 and won't give presentations to groups of more than 20 because those are the months he plans to write his next book and wants to spend time with his children during those months.

Jude has found it much simpler to say no to many of the many requests he receives for guest speaking now that he has developed his stringent criteria. As long as he knows the rules, he doesn't have to think about who should be an exception.

For those who find it tough to say "no," it's time for a new strategy: rejecting categories. Whenever someone asks you to do something for them, say no. Reject the request automatically and completely. You can always say yes if it's something you want to do. However, the answer "no" should be your first choice.

Preempting a request from someone who makes frequent requests is a good idea if you have them in your life. "I'm aware that you'll be moving at the end of the month. I'm afraid I'll have to pass on helping you move this time. My spouse and I decided that we needed to spend more time with our children."

"Yes. What can I prioritise less of?"

When you've got a lot on your plate, someone can ask you to do something that will just add to your workload. Whether at work, in public, or at home, if responding to their request will jeopardise your productivity, you must firmly refuse it. Despite this, it can still be difficult to say no, especially to individuals with authority, such as a supervisor or those we have deep affections for and are afraid to disappoint.

Another approach to say no in these instances is to say yes—with a catch. Ask them which of your many other obligations you can stop working on to create room for their request, and then agree.

This approach is ideal for scenarios in which you're answering to someone in a position of authority: "Sure, I'd be pleased to assist you in going through our budget for the upcoming year. To devote my full attention to that task, I need to clear my schedule. Should I put off the archive project or the marketing presentation for the time being?"

However, it works just as effectively in one's personal life. "A few things on my calendar interfere with helping you relocate this weekend: a family visit with my mother and the ballet recital of my daughter. What would you do if you were in my shoes?" "I can assist you with painting your living room as far as I know." "Is it more important to focus on cleaning up the garage or tending to the garden?"

Several factors make this strategy effective. Sending a positive message with your "yes" indicates a willingness to participate. Asking your requestor to select which items to skip for the time being gives the impression that they have a choice (while in reality, it is you making the decision)... To be honest, it's probably the best way to communicate, "I'm swamped right now." It shows that you aren't going to give in to their every whim and that you aren't going to give in.

With all of the things you've got going on, you're also establishing yourself as a systematic schedule-setter. Finally, you're establishing a personal boundary in the most dignified manner. Those are critical actions to take if you want to get out of people-pleasing mode.

Maintain simplicity

Saying no is easier when you keep it short and sweet. You can't learn how to do it; it's a natural reaction to the act itself. After a long period of inactivity, people will be startled when you tell them no. Those with an alpha personality will certainly try to sway you from your decision, so be prepared for that. It may be because of your lack of self-confidence that they gravitate toward you in the first place, and it's difficult to alter a long-standing dynamic. When you introduce a new dynamic, expect a backlash and astonishment.

In a situation like this, the last thing you want to do is go back and change your mind. Be aware that you'll have to deal with this person again and again if you decide to accept their request. They'll also be aware that you're open to modifying your refusal. Keep repeating the same thing over and over again. Don't give them a chance to argue by saying "no" every time they ask. Weakness in your position will only encourage individuals who want to persuade you further.

Don't give in to the temptation of the moment. Saying no is the hardest when you've already said it. At this point, you'll want to help, keep talking, or do whatever else to ease the tension that your no has caused. "Well, if you need my assistance, I'd be happy to lend a hand..." "I don't want to, but..." You're more likely to lose self-confidence if you speak up instead of keeping your mouth shut.

To say no without making excuses, realise that you don't. You can cite a variety of excuses, such as being overworked or lacking expertise, but that's it. That's all there is to it. Don't get bogged down in unnecessary details if you still feel the need to include a "because" after your statement. The more information you provide, the more food for thought it becomes for those who will pick through it. Even if you tell someone that you can't help with a friend's move so that you may go for a walk with your cat first thing in the morning, they may argue that you don't need to walk your cat at all.

Don't waste your time with a meaningless explanation for why you rejected the offer. Be honest and don't need to explain why you turned down the opportunity. It's quite acceptable to decline an offer. There's no need to elaborate further. It's important to remember that "no" can be used as a full phrase.

Hoops can be made. You can put the decision off until later or delay it indefinitely as an alternative to saying no. Then, ask them if they can do anything to help you prepare for the possibility of it happening. Put the responsibility on them by demanding that they assist you in considering their proposal. Confused?

Let's look at David, a brilliant entrepreneur who also serves as a mentor. People who want to "pick his brain" and learn from him like a sponge frequently approach him for coffee. As you might expect, he does not have the time to respond to everyone who contacts him. He has to say "no" a lot, but he has figured out a way around it. Before he agrees to anything else, he sets up a hurdle for them to jump past. His preferred method of inviting someone over to his house is by email, and when they do so, he'll ask them to provide him with a plan outlining what they want to talk about and why. Only a small percentage of the persons he met are ever heard from again.

As David's instance demonstrates, those who only wish to take advantage of you without making it easy can be seen. If someone begs for anything from you, set a requirement that they must meet before you consider their request. Because they'd have to put in the time and effort, most people will never get back to you!

"I'm not sure right now, but I would appreciate it if you could follow up with me." When someone else is responsible for something, the best-case scenario is that they either forget about it or are lazy and don't do anything. This, of course, is the same as passing the load onto someone else. "I can't right now, but maybe when my circumstances improve," is another option.

A ruse of deception, "I can't do that, but I can do this," is another choice if you're having difficulty saying no. "You can count on me to help you relocate for two hours, but I won't be able to do it all day long." Or try, "I sincerely intend to spend time with you during the next month even if I am unable to do it this weekend."

"Though I cannot serve on the board, I am available for ad hoc consultation anytime you need it." To say no and then offer a smaller consolation award may or may not be accepted is what you're doing here. Although it may be a viable solution if you are prepared to do it, it is not required.

Your no is hidden because you appear open and willing on the surface. People are more likely to reject and advise you not to bother if you offer something tiny. An even better approach is to supply as little information as possible and let the reader draw their conclusions. Freedom from a demand or an obligation is almost always achieved through bait and switch. Because you're saying yes to something but not what's being asked, this strategy reduces anxiety to a great extent.

Don't make it personal. When we say no, we often feel bad because we know how it would feel to be rejected. We can think that someone doesn't care about us or that the symbolism is lacking because of it. As a result, it is critical to keep your no as non-personal as possible and focused on the current circumstance.

In other words, you're not rejecting the individual because of who they are as a person, but rather because of their predicament. Even though some people find it difficult to distinguish between the two, the former is considerably simpler to understand and hear.

Imagine being invited to a friend's party, only to find out that your ex will be there with whom you had a particularly ugly breakup. It's not about your friend; it's about the situation and that you're in a confined space with someone who makes you nauseous. Rather than saying no to spending time with your friend, as they would think, you would underline that you are saying no to being in the presence of your ex.

"I'd really like to, and I was looking forward to hanging out with you, but I can't!" is a good example of regret. People are more likely to accept a no if they feel validated rather than rejected. Be careful to concentrate on the situation's specifics and why it will not benefit you.

The blame is yours. You're not saying "no," but rather "Yes, but... Allow me to explain what I mean." To "pass the buck" is to delegate the burden of accountability to someone else.

Because someone else would be a far better match for the position, it's a sign that you should resign. Even if you wouldn't be doing justice to the requester, you can still aid them by finding a solution to their problem. The most crucial component is that the requester will not hear a no.

Think of it this way: If you ask for a ride to the airport because you are nervous about driving on the motorway, you may answer, "No thanks, I'm a terrible driver, and Ted is a terrific driver and could be free that day!" You've successfully delegated responsibility to Ted by reducing yourself to nothingness in the face of Ted's potential solutions.

When someone asks you for anything, it's usually to help them with a difficulty they're facing. As long as you can point them on the right path, you've avoided a responsibility if you appear to be a bad option but point them on the right route.

It is important to know how to say no. You'll manage your life and your time better if you learn to say no. You'll be better able to avoid doing things you don't want to do if you can learn to say no. When you know how to say no, you're less likely to cause conflict and upset others. If you don't say "no," you're living someone else's life instead of your own.

The ability to say no, like any other skill, may be learned. It's possible for you, too, to learn to say no. After some practice, you'll wonder what to do with all the time you'll have after you're a pro at saying no.

As previously stated, there will be at least some repercussions for standing your ground. Even if you employ some of the more inventive methods discussed in this chapter, you'll find yourself saying no more and more.

As a result of your lack of regular contact, some of the individuals you've always been able to satisfy may take offence. They've gotten used to you just doing what they want and not protesting.

Because you've changed that dynamic, you should brace yourself for some immediate backlash.

As with setting boundaries, your anger will subside over time and perhaps transform into respect. You won't simply be perceived as someone eager to please others, but as someone responsible, organised, and intentional.

Conclusion

You've done it. Hopefully, you've gained the confidence to live out the purpose for which you were put on this earth. Full, magnificent, quirky, courageous, and distinctive, you are strongly connected to your passion, skills, and ability to positively impact others. The work you've done so far brings you closer than ever before, so don't be afraid to believe in your ability to get there.

There's a lot of work to do and new things to discover in your life. Using this guidebook will help you get to where you want to go. Your goal is to overcome your fear and have the courage to be different. Dig deep and genuinely comprehend how fear has trapped you to achieve this goal. You'll also have to think about what kind of life you want to lead.

New experiences, hardships, and self-discovery are all part of any journey. You can embark on this path alone or with the help of a family member, friend, or counsellor. According to most people, the support of others can be extremely beneficial while taking on new difficulties. Your trip may be exhilarating, demanding, and even frightening at times. But it will all be worth it when you can make significant changes in your life and have more freedom in your daily routines.

Put an end to the paralysing effects of dread by taking action today! It's time to face your fears and phobias head-on and have the courage to be different. You are capable of achieving your goals.

Feedback

Thank you for reading 'Have The Courage To Be Different'. I sincerely hope you enjoyed and got value from this book, and that it helps you to forge those all-important positive habits that will bring peace and harmony to your life from this moment on.

If you have a free moment, please leave me some feedback on Amazon.

Also, scan the QR code below to visit the Hackney and jones Publishing website where you can find more information on the range of books available.

HackneyandJones.com

Printed in Great Britain
by Amazon